PRAISE FOR AGAINST HAPPINESS

"Mr. Wilson's case for the dark night of the soul brings a much needed corrective to today's mania for cheerfulness. One would almost say that, in its eloquent contrarianism and earnest search for meaning, *Against Happiness* lifts the spirits."
—COLIN McGINN, *The Wall Street Journal*

"[Wilson has] the passionate soul of a nineteenth-century romantic who, made wise by encounters with his own personal darkness, invites readers to share his reverence for nature and exuberance for life. Providing a powerful literary complement to recent psychological discussions of melancholy... this selection is variously gloomy and ecstatic, infuriating and even inspiring."
—BRENDAN DRISCOLL, *Booklist*

"An impassioned, compelling, dare I say poetic, argument on behalf of those who 'labor in the fields of sadness'... A loose and compelling argument for fully embracing one's existence, for it is a miracle itself—a call to live hard and full, to participate in the great rondure of life and to be aware of the fact that no one perspective on the world is ever finally true."
—ETHAN RUTHERFORD, *Star Tribune* (Minneapolis)

"[A] lively, reasoned call for the preservation of melancholy in the face of all-too-rampant cheerfulness... Pithy and epigrammatic."   —BRIAN SHOLIS, *Bookforum*

"Wilson's argument is important, and he makes it with passion." —TODD SHY, *The News and Observer* (Raleigh)

"[A] potent little polemic . . . Poetic prose . . . If you think the world is being overrun by zombie Pollyannas intent on spreading their insidious joy, *Against Happiness* will gladden your heart." —LISA GABRIELE, *The Globe and Mail*

"A deeply philosophical polemic . . . Lucid and engaging prose." —SAM WELLER, *Playboy.com*

"A lucid, literate defense of feeling like hell—and, in fact, of feeling itself." —DAVID GATES, author of *Jernigan*

"I have never been Mr. Happy, but after reading *Against Happiness*, I felt a lot better about myself. It almost made me happy. An important book and a stunning reminder, in these troubled times, that there are important lessons in our pain and that a smile may make a better moment, but not a better world." —LEWIS BLACK, author of *Nothing's Sacred*

"This movingly written book will change your mind, and maybe your life, with its pitiless account of the value of happiness and the price we Americans pay for pursuing it so compulsively. It may help us stand up before it's too late and face our demons, by learning to love the melancholy realism and the creative powers that arise out of the darkness in our hearts." —RICHARD KLEIN, author of *Cigarettes Are Sublime*

© WFU/KEN BENNETT

ERIC G. WILSON

AGAINST HAPPINESS

Eric G. Wilson is the Thomas H. Pritchard Professor of English at Wake Forest University in Winston-Salem, North Carolina. The recipient of several important awards, including a National Humanities Center yearlong fellowship, he is the author of five books on the relationship between literature and psychology.

AGAINST HAPPINESS

In Praise of Melancholy

ERIC G. WILSON

SARAH CRICHTON BOOKS

Farrar, Straus and Giroux

New York

SARAH CRICHTON BOOKS
Farrar, Straus and Giroux
18 West 18th Street, New York 10011

Copyright © 2008 by Eric G. Wilson
All rights reserved

Printed in the United States of America
Published in 2008 by Sarah Crichton Books/Farrar, Straus and Giroux
First paperback edition, 2009

The Library of Congress has cataloged the hardcover edition as follows:
  Wilson, Eric G.
    Against happiness : in praise of melancholy / Eric G.
  Wilson—1st ed.
      p. cm.
    "Sarah Crichton books."
    ISBN-13: 978-0-374-24066-0 (hardcover : alk. paper)
    ISBN-10: 0-374-24066-3 (hardcover : alk. paper)
    1. Melancholy. 2. Creative ability. I. Title.
    [DNLM: 1. Depression—psychology. 2. Creativeness.
  3. Depression—history. 4. Drug Therapy—adverse effects.
  5. Literature. WM 171 W747a 2008]

BF575.M44W55 2008
152.4—dc22

                                              2007031699

Paperback ISBN-13: 978-0-374-53166-9
Paperback ISBN-10: 0-374-53166-8

Designed by Cassandra J. Pappas

www.fsgbooks.com

For Sandi and Una

Contents

Against Happiness

INTRODUCTION

. . . melancholy is a fearful gift.
What is it but the telescope of truth?
—GEORGE GORDON, LORD BYRON

OURS ARE ominous times. Each nervous glance portends some potential disaster. Paranoia most mornings shocks us to wakefulness, and we totter out under the ghostly sun. At night fear agitates the darkness. Dreams of empty streets flitter through our fitful heads. Enduring these omens, as vague and elusive as the obscure horror they suggest, we strain to think of exactly what scares us. Our minds run over a daunting litany of global problems. We hope with our listing to find a meaning, a clue to our unease.

We mentally scan the scene. We are currently emitting too much carbon dioxide into the atmosphere. This gas traps the heat of the sun and thus raises the globe's temperature. Even as I write, the polar ice caps are melting. Within decades we could face major oceanic flooding. Even our greatest skyscrapers, yearning heavenward, could soon be devoured by indifferent waves. We are also close to annihilating hundreds of exquisite animals. These beasts—white rhinos and Sumatran tigers and California condors—have been in the making for millions of years. Within almost a human lifetime our disregard for nature has put these sublime creatures almost into extinction. Soon our forests will be empty of colorful torsos and exotic wings. These formerly teeming groves will be as bland as pavement. Moreover, we now find ourselves on the verge of a new cold war. Nuclear warheads before long will be on the rise again. The fears of the middle of the last century will return. We'll wonder: Will this year be the last that humans breathe and walk on this time-rending earth?

I can now add another threat, perhaps as dangerous as the most apocalyptic of concerns. We are possibly not far away from eradicating a major cultural force, a serious inspiration to invention, the muse behind much art and poetry and music. We are wantonly hankering to rid the world of numerous ideas and visions, multitudinous innovations and meditations. We are right at this moment annihilating melancholia.

We wonder if the wide array of antidepressants will one day make sweet sorrow a thing of the past. We wonder if soon enough every single American will be happy. We wonder if we will become a society of self-satisfied smiles. Treacly expressions will be painted on our faces as we parade through the pastel aisles. Bedazzling neon will spotlight our way.

What is behind this desire to purge sadness from our

lives, especially in America, the land of splendid dreams and wild success? Why are most Americans so utterly willing to have an essential part of their hearts sliced away and discarded like so much waste? What are we to make of this American obsession with happiness, an obsession that could well lead to a sudden extinction of the creative impulse, that could result in an extermination as horrible as those foreshadowed by global warming and environmental crisis and nuclear proliferation? What drives this rage for complacency, for the innocuous smile? What fosters this desperate contentment?

These questions of course cut against the grain of what most Americans claim to think. A recent poll conducted by the Pew Research Center shows that almost 85 percent of Americans believe that they are very happy or at least happy. The psychological world is now abuzz with a new field, positive psychology, devoted to finding ways to enhance happiness through pleasure, engagement, and meaning. Psychologists practicing this brand of therapy are leaders in a novel sort of science, the science of happiness. Mainstream publishers are now learning from the self-help industry and printing thousands of books on how to be happy and on why we are happy. The self-help press fills the shelves with step-by-step plans for worldly satisfaction. Everywhere I see advertisements offering even more happiness, happiness on land or by sea, in a car or under the stars. And as I have already noted, doctors now offer a wide array of drugs that might eradicate depression forever. It seems truly, perhaps more than ever before, an age of almost perfect contentment, a brave new world of persistent good fortune, joy without trouble, felicity with no penalty.

Surely all this happiness can't be for real. How can so many people be happy in the midst of all the problems that beset our globe—not only the collective and apocalyptic ills just mentioned but also those particular irritations that bedevil our everyday existences, those money issues and marital spats, those stifling vocations and lonely dawns? Are we to believe that four out of every five Americans can be content amid the general woe? Are some people lying, or are they simply afraid to be honest in a culture in which the status quo is nothing short of manic bliss? Aren't we suspicious of this statistic? Aren't we further troubled by our culture's overemphasis on happiness? Don't we fear that this rabid focus on exuberance leads to half-lives, to bland existences, to wastelands of mechanistic behavior?

I for one am afraid that our American culture's overemphasis on happiness at the expense of sadness might be dangerous, a wanton forgetting of an essential part of a full life. I further am wary in the face of this possibility: to desire only happiness in a world undoubtedly tragic is to become inauthentic, to settle for unrealistic abstractions that ignore concrete situations. I am finally fearful over our society's efforts to expunge melancholia from the system. Without the agitations of the soul, would all of our magnificently yearning towers topple? Would our heart-torn symphonies cease?

I want to get to the bottom of these fears, to see if they're legitimate or just neurotic grumblings. My feeling right now is that they are valid. This sense grows out of my suspicion that the predominant form of American happiness breeds blandness. This kind of happiness appears to entertain a craven disregard for the value of sadness. This brand of supposed joy, moreover, seems to foster an ongoing ignorance of life's enduring and vital polarity between agony and ecstasy, dejection and ebulliance. Trying to forget sadness and its integral place in the great rhythm of the cosmos, this sort of happiness insinuates in the end that the blues are an aberrant state that should be cursed as weakness of will or removed with the help of a little pink pill.

Let me be clear. I'm right now thinking only of this specific American type of happiness. I'm not questioning joy in general. For instance, I'm not challenging that unbearable exuberance that suddenly emerges from long suffering. I'm not troubled by that hard-earned tranquillity that comes from long meditation on the world's sorrows. I'm not criticizing that slow-burning bliss that issues from a life spent helping those that hurt.

Likewise, I'd like to be clear about this: I don't want to romanticize clinical depression. I realize that there are many lost souls out there who require medication to keep from killing themselves or harming their friends and families. I don't want to question the pharmaceutical therapies of the seriously depressed. Not only am I not qualified to do this (I'm not a psychotherapist marshaling evidence, but a literary humanist searching for a deeper life), I'm also not willing to argue against medications that simply make existence bearable for so many with biochemical disorders.

I do, however, wonder why so many people experiencing

melancholia are now taking pills meant simply to ease the pain, to turn scowls once more into smiles. Of course there is a fine line between what I'm calling melancholia and what society calls depression. In my mind, what separates the two is degree of activity. Both forms are more or less chronic sadness that leads to ongoing unease with how things are—persistent feelings that the world as it is is not quite right, that it is a place of suffering, stupidity, and evil. Depression (as I see it, at least) causes apathy in the face of this unease, lethargy approaching total paralysis, an inability to feel much of anything one way or another. In contrast, melancholia (in my eyes) generates a deep feeling in regard to this same anxiety, a turbulence of heart that results in an active questioning of the status quo, a perpetual longing to create new ways of being and seeing.

Our culture seems to confuse these two and thus treat melancholia as an aberrant state, a vile threat to our pervasive notions of happiness—happiness as immediate gratification, happiness as superficial comfort, happiness as static contentment. Of course the question immediately arises: Who wouldn't question this apparently hollow form of American happiness? Aren't all of us late at night, when we're honest with ourselves, opposed to shallow happiness? Most likely we are, but isn't it possible that many of us fall into superficiality without knowing it? Aren't some of us so smitten with the American dream that we have become brainwashed into believing that our sole purpose on this earth is to be happy? Doesn't this unwitting affection for happiness over sadness lead us to a one-sided life, to bliss without discomfort, bright noon with no night?

My sense is that most of us have been duped by the American craze for happiness. We might think that we're leading a truly honest existence, one attuned to vivid realities and blooded hearts, when we're really just behaving as predictably and artificially as robots, falling easily into well-worn "happy" behaviors, into the conventions of contentment, into obvious grins. Deceived, we miss out on the great interplay of the living cosmos, its luminous gloom, its terrible beauty.

The American dream might be a nightmare. What passes for bliss could well be a dystopia of flaccid grins. Our passion for felicity hints at an ominous hatred for all that grows and thrives and then dies—for all those curious thrushes moving among autumn's brownish indolence, for those blue dahlias seemingly hollowed with sorrow, for all those gloomy souls who long for clouds above high windows. I'd hate for us to awaken one morning and regret what we've done in the name of untroubled enjoyment. I'd hate for us to crawl out of our beds and walk out into a country denuded of gorgeous lonely roads and the grandeur of desolate hotels, of half-cracked geniuses and their frantic poems. I'd hate for us to come to consciousness when it's too late to live.

THE AMERICAN DREAM

May the sun in his course visit no land more free, more
happy, more lovely, than this our own country!
—DANIEL WEBSTER

IN THE WINTER of 1620 William Bradford's battered
and scarred ship—called, perhaps too hopefully, the
Mayflower—hit land at Cape Cod. Bradford and his fellow
passengers, mostly Protestant Separatists in search of religious freedom, were not ready for what they saw. There before their weary eyes was not what they had expected in this
new world, vibrant verdure and copious bounty. Instead,
threatening their sea-hardened gaze was a vast waste, cold
and inhospitable. Bradford described this scene in his journal. He noted how he and his companions had "now no
friends to welcome them, nor inns to entertain or refresh
their weather-beaten bodies, no houses or much less towns
to repair to, to seek for succor." To make matters worse, the
season was winter, and therefore "sharp and violent and sub-

ject to cruel and fierce storms." These vicious snows ravaged
"a hideous and desolate wilderness, full of wild beasts and
wild men." These religious pilgrims could not compare
themselves with Moses upon Mount Pisgah, the peak from
which the great prophet beheld the Promised Land, the
sweet land of milk and honey. These seekers could take comfort only in the mercy of heaven, for wherever they looked
on earth, they found "little solace or content in respect of
any outward objects." They knew that help could come only
from the "spirit of God and his grace."

Bradford and his peers wanted terribly to be like Moses.
Oppressed in Anglican England for their dissenting beliefs,
Bradford and the religious rebels he eventually led felt as
though they had been enslaved in Egypt. They dreamed of
their own exodus, a flight over an oceanic desert to a lush
land where they could worship their God as they saw fit.
Their expectation was keen, desperate; they believed that
America, that fresh and innocent country, would fulfill all
their desires for religious bliss. They thought that they
would on the American shore discover true happiness and
put most sadness to rout. When their hopes were destroyed
by the icy reality of the New England coast, they nonetheless persisted in their optimism. They held hard to a faith
that God would provide for them. They felt that they were a
blessed group. Instead of succumbing to melancholia before
harsh earthly sights, they turned their heads toward heaven.
There in the pale winter sky they envisioned a God who
would reward them properly for their labors. Their miraculous survival through those first few northern winters—

with the gracious aid of American natives—only bore out their faith. Their wild optimism in the end seemed valid, and for that unyielding confidence, that faith that happiness will always overcome sadness, we still yearly give fervid thanks.

This story of course stands as one of the earliest instances of American optimism. Even in the face of almost certain defeat, the so-called Pilgrims never faltered in their belief that God would reward them for their strenuous efforts. These pious men and women held in their heart of hearts the conviction that they had reached a place of destiny, a special environment fated to give them the happiness that they deserved. If they had to gaze above the bleak landscape to achieve this bright-eyed vision, then so be it.

Bradford's group was one of the first to sail to America in hopes of finding a form of happiness unavailable in oppressive Europe. The successive groups taking ship from Europe to America provides a not-so-secret history of the American mind, a look at America as a perennial land of desire, of crazed and compulsive hopefulness. By the end of the seventeenth century the eastern shores of America teemed with religious communities hungry for a utopia in the New World. Soon Americans with more secular aims began to mine the wilds for fungible products, to transform the unmapped world into unimaginable wealth. These early merchants quickly achieved great success, and thus a new call came to Europe from across the Atlantic: America is a land not only of religious freedom but also of free trade, of unprecedented financial opportunity, of worldly wealth. The cross had given way to the coin. But the fervor was still religious, faith in God turned into worship of gold.

If pious men like Bradford were the leaders of the seventeenth-century drive for religious utopia, prudent folks like Benjamin Franklin spearheaded the eighteenth-century push for financial security. In his numerous books, essays, and letters, Franklin persistently explored the path to riches, to happiness through transforming time into money. In the persona of Poor Richard in *The Way to Wealth* (1758), Franklin famously set down his pithy aphorisms on how to transform unruly time, shocking in each strange instant, into a series of predictable moneymaking moments. His goal throughout this little pamphlet was to urge Americans to manage their time, to take charge of their days. This control over the clock would turn each tick or tock into property.

It should not be surprising that Franklin worked on the Declaration of Independence. In this document, of course, we learn that everyone enjoys an inalienable right to "life, liberty, and the pursuit of happiness." What many of us don't know, though, is that "the pursuit of happiness" is secretly connected to the ownership of property. In his *Second Treatise of Civil Government* (1690), John Locke, the great British philosopher, claimed that everyone has a right to "life, liberty, and property." This statement lies behind the famous sentence in our declaration. This covert connection between happiness and property confirms what Franklin proposed throughout his work: the true road to earthly joy is through the accumulation of stuff. This was a convenient and welcome sentiment in a new country still famous for its immense unmapped spaces. These wide-open plains were raw materials just waiting for enterprising young men to transform them into dollars and delights. Trees were tender, and clouds, commerce.

Hidden, then, in the Declaration of Independence is the reason why so many folks past and present have come to America: it was and still is the place where one can find happiness through acquisition. The religious utopia has given way to the capitalistic paradise. In this paradise, curious creatures are transformed into quantifiable commodities. The outlandish, mysterious, sometimes turbulent world is turned into a safe surface, a smooth plain on which one can project his numerical fantasies. This is the method of capitalistic seeing, of American seeing. There in the distance, let us say, is a thriving forest, filled with yearning eagles and pines that tower, an occasional daisy and booming rapids. What is this to the typical American, the American bent on discovering happiness through securing stuff? This wooded region is not a robust ecosystem, a living organism in which parts nourish the whole and the whole fosters the parts. On the contrary, this forest is to the American entrepreneur a reservoir of resources, a space containing materials just waiting to be bought and sold. This American does not see the forest at all, its bizarre breathings and beautiful wreaths. All he views are numbers, price tags, and savings bonds. He trades quality for quantity. He thus loses reality.

In this way the capitalist of Franklin is little different from the Puritan of Bradford. Both overlook the real, the howling wilderness and the holy wood, in hopes of resting in security—in the eternal bosom of God, in the durable dirt of purchased land. In their desire to discover perfect happiness in a world that jostles between jaundice and euphoria, these American types must necessarily send their gaze into the vagaries of heaven or the abstractions of numbers. This is the basis of the American dream: the trading of the quick buzz and hum of the real for the placid structures of sound institutions. The dream of the American is the death of the actual.

There is more to this. To see through the lenses of God's heaven or the bank's harmony is in the end to witness the world only through a narcissistic perspective. If I reduce my teeming environment to a strategy for salvation or a plan for savings, then I perceive the landscape only through the windows of my own desire for perfect happiness, for total security and contentment. In other words, I see only what fits into the grids of my own mind, networks devoted solely to my personal comfort. I'm not interested in the objective world. I am attuned only to those parts that I can transform into material to boost my ego. Wherever I look, I experience myself. I flatten the vast universe into a small round mirror onto which I project my blissful visions. I see surrounding me, whether I'm on mountain or sea, my own grimaced grin.

OUR RECENT CULTURE HAS made it startlingly easy to live only in a world of personal dreams, a realm from which hard reality has largely been vanquished. It is our cutting-edge technologies that have empowered us to shape the world into a paradise of convenience and efficiency. With our computers and our medical machines and our pharmaceuticals in tow, we appear to have very little to worry about beyond our next quick fix.

We need not look far to see our artificial culture in action. Thanks to the digital age, we are more likely to witness pixels than people. We spend hours in front of our PCs playing in the wispy fields of virtual reality. In the infinite corridors of the Internet, we find Web pages more interesting than the morning strands, shiny with dew, of the garden spider. Indeed, we treat our machine as if it were an organ and our organs as if they were machines. Our computer can be "user friendly." It can come down with a "virus." Meanwhile we engage in "interfaces" with our colleagues. We "process" ideas.

We spend our times away from the PC getting high on our BlackBerrys or cell phones, which provide immediate satiation of our desires for information and communication. We don't have to wait even a second to get right before our eyes the latest scores and highlights or the important messages from our friends or parents. Why should we even go to games or meet actual people when all that is alive—from graceful skaters to wizened professors—can be translated into megabytes and compressed into a screen the size of a matchbox? We carry with us the world wherever we go; we don't need to go anywhere.

Our high-definition televisions, hooked up to satellites and cables that put thousands of channels at our fingertips, grant us access immediately to whatever images we want. I can lounge in my den at noon, eating a burrito and dreaming of a new shade of blue, and suddenly before my eyes, on my television, comes an image on channel 176, an azure dome from Burma. Though I sit on my couch in a dim room consuming microwavable food, I can find my bright visions realized not through motion or effort but simply through breathing before my plasma television, fake blood that gives me false reality.

If these diversions aren't enough to satisfy our whims, then we have medical technologies to ensure that we get artificial health. If we are too wired to sleep after our day of surfing the Net and tapping out text messages, then we can pop an Ambien or a Lunesta to give us artificially induced sleep. If we're feeling just a little blue, a bit off-kilter, psychologically speaking, we can take Paxil or Prozac and in a few days enjoy an unreal gratification, the two-beer buzz of canned bliss. What if you've been overindulging lately on PowerBars and pork rinds? Not to worry. For a decent fee you can pay for liposuction and tummy tucking to offer the look of health.

In each of these cases we have traded flesh for prosthetics, heart for hardware. But none of this should be surprising, given the capitalistic view with which we've been brought up. From an early age we are taught to translate the creatures around us—though they be toads that glisten or mica shining at noon—into clean surfaces on which we can project our dreams of total happiness. In this American capitalistic view the world is a kind of vast playground, with each object serving its purpose for pleasure. Who cares if what we normally call reality is forsaken? Who minds if the rich interplay between growth and decay, ecstasy and agony is reduced to only one side of the pole, to the flat line of life without death and joy without turbulence? As long as we're happy, what's the point of complaining? Aren't we put on earth to be happy? Isn't it a great victory, then, to be able to make the world say yes at every turn, indeed to value only those parts that tickle our fancies? We are gods of a pleasure dome of our own making.

REALLY, what's lost in all of this? Isn't it a mark of our American genius that we can now envision a cosmos of total contentment, a universe in which all the things that chagrin us, from depression to corpulence, from distance to death, might soon simply fade away? We have finally created that perfect utopia about which Bradford dreamed and Franklin schemed. We are smoothing over the rough edges of aging. We are transforming dirty cities into massive shopping malls. We have even translated war into blips on our television screens. There is no better time to play at living. No wonder almost every American claims to be happy.

We likely feel that we have finally come fully into our American birthright. For years our parents have told us that America is the country where we can be anything we want to be. Before we even have bootstraps, or know what they are, we think that we can pull ourselves up by them, that we can transform ourselves from suffering adolescents to powerful presidents. Our technologically efficient culture makes these opinions all the easier to hold, for our gadgets increasingly push anything like reality into the background. We can substitute our dreams for data, our desires for death. Everywhere we look, we see the big yellow smiley face. Everywhere we listen, we hear "Have a nice day." Everywhere we breathe is the smell of plastic. To be a patriot is to be peppy. The citizen is felicitous.

Indeed, in my experience some of our most sacred institutions have become happiness schools. In the university where I teach, this is sometimes so. While the liberal arts education was once a studious course emphasizing the intrinsic value of education, it is now mostly a precursor to trade. American education is largely a preparation for American capitalism. The long, sonorous, and somber sentences of Herman Melville become quips for the cocktail party. Nietzsche's joyous tragedy turns into the butt of a well-placed joke on European dourness. The precise science of economics translates into sloppy personal supply and demand: I need a Beemer to be happy, and I shall provide the labor, whatever it is, to get it. Psychology, that plumb line into the profound depths of personality, converts to a shallow analysis of character types, a way of predicting what one's business partners will or will not do.

My experience in the Protestant church has been largely the same. Once the Protestant church was a place where one would grow to understand his severe optical limitations in comparison with the infinite vision of a ubiquitous deity, a God whose center is everywhere and circumference nowhere. Now, at least in my eyes, the numerous churches devoted to Baptists, Methodists, Presbyterians, Lutherans, and the like are basically happiness companies, corporations that focus on how one can achieve blessedness while living in this world. In the pews and pulpits, contrition has turned trite, and contentment has become the given. The blessed gaze of those striding from the aisles to the vestibule is inspiring to behold. The firm farewell handshake between the minister and his parishioner is a sacred seal, a bond: stay happy until next week, for God has planned for you to prosper, if only you will pray over your repasts and tithe your earnings.

My sense of politics is the same. Formerly an arena in which the difficult principles of democracy were debated and validated, politics has now become entertainment. We can turn on the television any night of the week and witness shrill political pundits argue their dogma. Or we can engage in that most pleasurable of sports: mocking the pomposity of political speeches, filled as they are with worn clichés and vapid promises. We turn the political process to commodity, an object for enjoyable consumption. Democracy becomes dumb, and we blithely cheer its increasing demise.

What, then, is America becoming? It is turning into a nation of true consumers, people bent on taking in huge mouthfuls of Happy Meals, hoping too for the special prize, earned just for eating an imitation of a real hamburger. What, really, could be wrong with this? Apparently a lot could be wrong. Look at what sort of people this culture is creating. I have seen them. You have too. They haunt the gaudy and garish spaces of the world and ignore the dark margins.

They tilt their heads to the side, feign bemusement, and nod knowingly. They clinch their eyes in looks of concern. They blink a lot, bewildered. They murmur truisms about overcoming adversity. They say that they love their parents and puppies and all babies. They devour bestsellers about the wisdom of children or coaches. They can be smarmy warmongering conservatives or passive-aggressive peace-loving liberals. They can be Christians hiding their meanness or New Agers hungry for power. They adore the Lifetime channel. They are happy campers. They want God to bless the world. They want us to ask them about their children. They believe that a hug is an ideal gift; one size fits all. They think that kind words make good echoes. They join Book-of-the-Month clubs and identify with sympathetic characters. They sign their e-mails with chirpy icons. They swear by the power of prayer. They swear by the power of positive thinking. They dream of having Norman Vincent Peale as a dinner guest. They would eat Jell-O and Cool Whip. They would eat turkey too and make an endless Thanksgiving.

I THINK THAT by now we are beginning to see that this American quest for happiness at any cost is not merely a pastime, an occasional undertaking. We are starting to realize that this push for earthly bliss is at the core of the American soul. But we are also on the verge of comprehending something else again: this quest for happiness at the expense of sadness, this obsession with joy without tumult, is dangerous, a deeply troubling loss of the real, of that interplay, rich and terrific, between antagonisms. What are the consequences of this loss? Where does this endless drive for good cheer leave us?

Initially, we probably fear that this hunger for happiness at the expense of sadness is somehow unnatural, a violation of how the cosmos conducts itself. Again, what is existence if not an enduring polarity, an endless dance of limping dogs and lilting crocuses, starlings that are spangled and frustrated worms? Grasping onto one side of this perpetual antagonism between opposites, trying to experience happiness without gloom, is akin to wanting the sun to shine all the time, wishing only for winter, or yearning for up with no down. Think again of Bradford in the wilderness. He didn't pause on the possibility that the howling waste was a foil for his vision of heavenly escape. He didn't consider that he could not have envisioned salvation if not for his suffering. Remember also Franklin's Poor Richard. In translating all experiences into opportunities to make money, he forgets that dearth is the sibling of prosperity. Surely we don't want to settle for this one-sided world, this lopsided existence. Surely we want to develop full and capacious hearts capable of experiencing waste and water.

If we don't foster comprehensive hearts such as these, then we run the risk of living as abstractions, phantoms, ghosts with no gusto for life. If we want happiness at the expense of sadness, then we necessarily expect every tormented moment to yield nothing but new bliss. To keep this expectation alive, an expectation doomed to fail in the conflicted world, we must fixate on abstractions that have little to do with the concrete situation. We must hold hard to a concept of personal happiness over against a universe indifferent to our comfort. Holding tightly to this concept, we reduce the heterogeneous and nuanced universe to an idea, a narrow idea growing from our own selfish desire. No matter what I perceive, I labor to exact a suitable and pleasant meaning. I endeavor to see only what I want to see. I don't let the irreducibly strange and sorrowful world, replete with twisted turnips and elks that are wounded, rip me from my staid habits and throw me into profound meditation and significant action. In worshiping happiness, I blind myself to the planet.

This idea is beautifully expressed by Ralph Waldo Emerson, the great American essayist from the nineteenth century. In his essay "Experience" (1844), written soon after his firstborn child, Waldo, had succumbed to scarlet fever at the age of six, Emerson questions those who expect the world to rise to their overly optimistic expectations and extols the contrary sentiment: to anticipate nothing from the cosmos is to experience the vital interplay of oppositions as well as their golden mean. As Emerson writes: "I compared notes with one of my friends who expects everything of the universe and is disappointed when anything is less than the best, and I found that I begin at the other extreme, expecting nothing, and am always full of thanks for moderate goods. I accept the clangor and jangle of contrary tendencies. I find my account in sots and bores also . . . Everything good is on the highway. The middle region of our being is the temperate zone."

I'm not saying that all folks questing only for satisfaction are so shallow as to ignore the horrors of war or general pain. I am, though, suggesting this: a person seeking sleek comfort in this mysteriously mottled world—where love is always edged with resentment and baseness beds with grace—is necessarily required to perceive only small parts of the planet, those parts that fit into his preconceived mental grids. These grids allow in only data that reinforce a narrow sense of correctness. The grid keeper repeatedly intones: heaven has its God, and in the world all must be right.

All of us, of course, no matter how melancholy or not, are controlled by our preconceptions, by the abstractions that rule our minds. But some people strain all the time to break through their mental manacles, to cleanse the portals of their perceptions, and to see the universe as an ungraspable riddle, gorgeous and gross. Happy types, those Americans bent only on happiness and afraid of sadness, tend to forgo this labor. They sit safe in their cages. The sad ones, dissatisfied with the status quo, are more likely to beat against the bars.

Keen on turning each instant into an opportunity for new happiness, these happy types tend to become predictable. They frequently respond to different events in the same manner. Each day, crowded though it is with monumental tragedy, is "great." Every view from a battered yet indomitable mountain peak is "nice." Every person, even if he exudes rancor, is "a character." These reactions can become as regular as clockwork. When we are around people like this—and they seem to be legion—we long for some difference in rejoinder, some slight tremor that there's someone there, someone torn with bitterness or bent on mischief, aching over a mistake or just plain mean. We chafe at this endless repetition of cultural clichés, at this echo chamber of tired phrases, at this somewhat mechanical managing of abstraction.

We perhaps could be gentle toward these happy American types if their dreams were only abstract and predictable. But isn't there something else at work here, something potentially more pernicious? These dreams are ultimately delusional, and narcissistically so. Lopping off half the world with their one-sided responses, these American seekers of happiness are in danger of deluding themselves into believing that only one part of the world exists, the part that gladdens their egos. Entertaining this peril, these happy types really see only themselves. They colonize experience. They impose their imperialist egos onto the world. They reduce difference to the same.

There is of course something soul-deadening about being overly in love with oneself. When a person views the world only through his own experience, he divorces himself from the polarized flow of existence, that persistent dialogue between self and other, familiar and unfamiliar. Doing so, he fixates on constancy in the face of change, stasis against the kinetic motion of the cosmos. Isn't this a kind of death, an addiction to a sort of psychological rigor mortis? We wonder, then, if the obsession with happiness is, at the end of the day, a kind of unknowing necrophilia. We wonder if the desire for security is a hope for permanence, and we wonder if this hope for unchangeableness is a yen for death, the ultimate security blanket.

In his 1794 *The Book of Urizen*, William Blake, a British visionary poet of the late eighteenth and nineteenth centuries, profoundly sums up this connection between egocentric happiness and the secret desire for death. Famous for intoning that "the tygers of wrath are wiser than the horses of instruction," Blake in this poem argues that a person bent on living in a rationally predictable universe must necessarily desire a "solid without fluctuation" and a "joy without pain." These yearnings for complete security create a world of psychological stasis, a mental wasteland where nothing moves and lives. Wherever this person of total order looks, he sees only his own static thoughts projected outward. He does not perceive the thriving, spontaneous, contingent universe at all. He witnesses his brittle ego as in a mirror. As Blake says in another work, "There Is No Natural Religion" (1794), a man controlled by an overly rational yen for control sees "only Himself," while he who "sees the Infinite in all things, sees God." In other words, the person open to the unpredictable and unbounded nature of the world will open himself to an experience of ultimate reality, be it God or spirit or soul or energy or whatnot.

IN THE END it all comes down, does it not, to control? Don't people bent only on happiness, consumed with the American dream, wish for control of life? They hope to be able to call the shots, to punch their own tickets, to do it their own way. Of course on some level all of us, no matter whether we are happy or sad, desire control over our destiny. The problem comes, we might say, in desiring too much control, in yearning for the world to yield to our will. Those after complete happiness very likely wish for complete autonomy, the ability to transport life's inevitable shocks to some ethereal plane from which they can pick and choose whatever meanings they wish to endorse. This distant place is unreal, unseemly, scared. The happy man is the hollow man.

Ensconced in their solipsistic silos, these American happy types are hopelessly frustrated because they're trying desperately for security in an insecure world. They diligently attempt to control slippery time, but the whizzing minutes always elude their grasp. Still, they try to convince themselves that they are nonetheless catching and molding each tick of the clock. They are doomed to hold sieves; they believe they have buckets. This tension between belief and reality gives them hard edges around their smiles. Though they hold hard to their delusion, underneath, unconsciously, they probably know that they have no more control of their lives than a pebble in the rough currents of the river.

Alan Watts gets all this right in his 1951 *The Wisdom of Insecurity*. In this little book on the dangers of wanting control in an uncontrollable world, he claims that "there is a contradiction in wanting to be perfectly secure in a universe whose very nature is momentariness and fluidity." This contradiction leads those bent on control into an excruciating double bind. These types overly enamored of security spend much of their energy trying to "make permanent those experiences and joys which are only lovable because they are changing." In attempting to make impermanent joys—dying roses, growing children—stable, these controlling sorts of people actually alienate themselves from what they most want to embrace. If these folks could relinquish their desire for security, then they would ironically experience a kind of stability, the enduring polarities that organize the universe. To hope for a happiness that's secure is to fall into terrible insecurity, a feeling of divorce from the world's rhythms. To want a state that unpredictably oscillates between sadness and joy is to discover predictable dualities. Performing the happy life is giving over to artifice. Enduring the sad existence is participating in life's vital rhythms. Pallid happiness is here hell, and melancholia, dark, is the way to earthly heaven.

That's finally it; happy types ultimately don't live their own lives at all. They follow some prefabricated script, some ten-step plan for bliss or some stairway to heaven. Doing so, they separate themselves from the present moment, immediate and unrepeatable and pressing. They live in the past, holding sentimentally to the affirmations handed down by their parents or priests or self-help gurus, or they live in the future, hoping for the perfection they deserve, that they've been living all of their days to realize.

Driven by a desire for happiness at the expense of sadness, bolstered by capitalistic seeing and virtual reality, obsessed with abstraction and delusion, most of us are walking around half blind. Does this blindness partially account for a recent study, reported in *Psychological Science*, that found that happy people are more likely to be bigots than sad people? Does this inability to see clearly further account for the fact, revealed in the 2006 Pew Report on Social Trends, that Republicans, who can be a somewhat warlike bunch, are happier than Democrats? Is our nation's happiness, its crass self-satisfaction, its wretched contentment, partially responsible for its getting behind a recent war that never should have occurred?

LET'S BE SERIOUS, we all know people who mostly or at least partially fit these descriptions. We know that deep down they're frustrated, these happy types, these types that struggle to avoid melancholia. We know that on some level they're sick of shadows. We understand that they've missed many shocking scenes of the real. They've probably never moved among autumn's multihued lustrousness, through the serrated forms of orange and amber and crimson, with hearts irreparably ripped. They've probably not stared steadily at the sparrow lying stiff on the soiled snow. They've not walked by a nocturnal mirror and been stunned by the face they saw.

We also suspect that these happy types must live largely through repression. To strive to be happy all the time is necessarily to repress inevitable sadness. The persistent intoning of "I'm fine," "I'm fine" pushes down the gloom. There in the unconscious the dark feelings fester. They of course will not stay down but always will return in monstrous forms—in neurotic behaviors like constant hand washing or cleaning, in vicious nightmares and unseemly reveries. The problem is that these poor souls won't be aware of the source of their nervousness. They'll tend to blame others or the world, anything to keep intact the delusion that they're just fine, thank you, anything to keep at bay the vicious fear eating at their hearts.

We believe, then, that these happy types tend to suffer a desperate satisfaction. This of course leads to guilt. They look around everywhere and see others behaving as if they were perfectly happy. Yes, as the 2006 Pew Report showed, almost 85 percent of Americans claim to be happy. Those suffering the inner torment wonder what's wrong, why they can't get with the program, why they can't just get on board. They feel inadequate but must nonetheless lie to themselves and say everything's okay.

Forsaking these unrealistic expectations, happy types could for once face the agonized yet ecstatic contraries of life. They could realize that there is no joy without sorrow, no vivacious sun without the pockmarked moon. If they could understand this hard fact, deep, deep in their bones, then they could accept the scrambling of the cosmos, its ramming and slamming of opposing yet interdependent potencies. Suddenly sadness would not seem an aberration but instead a vital power, the enabler of joy. In a blink, delight would seem not the ideal state but only one pole of a vibrant continuum. Such transformations would trade timid comfort for furious exuberance. Such conversions would turn against happiness to be near ecstasy.

While millions of Americans have followed the happy

visions of Bradford and Franklin, there have been other Americans who have grounded their lives on a countertradition. This tradition views the fixation on happiness as a mark of superficiality and in turn sees the embrace of sadness as a token of profundity. The American exemplars of this alternative current are few but powerful. One such icon of this melancholy trend is Herman Melville, the author of that paean to woeful wisdom, *Moby-Dick*.

In 1856, Melville, melancholy and alone, made his way to the deserts of Egypt and Palestine. By this time in his career he was an outcast, a failed literary man. His masterpiece on the white whale, only five years old, was already gathering dust on forgotten bookshelves. His subsequent books were critical and commercial disasters. His appetite for worldly embrace unrequited, he set out for the ancient sands. Like his fellow exile Ishmael, he hoped to find sustenance amid the indifferent dunes.

In the course of his journey he stopped in England to visit his friend Nathaniel Hawthorne. The great maker of the gloomy *Scarlet Letter* was at the time serving as American consul in Liverpool. Hawthorne later described Melville's visit in his notebook. During a walk together along the Irish Sea, Melville had told him that he had "pretty much made up his mind to be annihilated." Hawthorne comments: "[B]ut still he does not seem to rest in that anticipation; and, I think, will never rest until he gets hold of a definite belief." With Melville's restlessness still in his mind, Hawthorne continues: "It is strange how he persists—and has persisted ever since I knew him, and probably long before—in wandering to and fro over these deserts, as dismal and monotonous as the sand hills amid which we were sitting." It is Melville's terrible doubt concerning the universe that inspires this nomadic life: "He can neither believe, nor be comfortable in his unbelief; and he is too honest and courageous not to try to do one or the other. If he were a religious man, he would be one of the most truly religious and reverential; he has a very high and noble nature, and better worth immortality than most of us."

Hawthorne here captures exactly what made Melville melancholy for most of his life: his inability to rest in a secure belief. Though this persistent skepticism might lead to an ongoing gloom, it nonetheless keeps the mind and the heart keen, active, alive. In his sublime volume on whale-torn waves, Melville imbues his main character, Ishmael, precisely with these traits. It is melancholia that inspires this fictional young man to take to ship. Floating there on those eternally inhumane oscillations, Ishmael broods constantly over the things of the universe—their appearances and their realities, their surfaces and their depths, their mysteries and revelations. One of his primary themes, one that he returns to again and again, is the connection between sadness and profundity.

When Ishmael first sees the *Pequod*, the hoary vessel in which he is to go a-whaling, he remarks that the ship is a most "noble craft, but somehow a most melancholy!" But then he concludes that all "noble things are touched with that." When Ishmael later analyzes the character of his captain, the grandly tragic Ahab, he notes the man's tormented and "moody stricken" face, a face with "all the nameless regal overbearing dignity of some mighty woe." Even later in the novel, Ishmael continues to ponder this connection between melancholia and grandeur. Witnessing the dark impulses of his fellow crew members, he is moved to say this: "So, therefore, that mortal man who hath more of joy than sorrow in him, that mortal man cannot be true—not true, or undeveloped." He goes on to say the same about books. He highlights the biblical Ecclesiastes, famous for intoning, "All is vanity," as "the fine hammered steel of woe." However, while he believes that there is a "woe that is wisdom," he also knows that too much woe can breed madness. The goal, he claims, is to find a dynamic balance between the darkness and the light, woe and good humor. He symbolizes this golden mean by invoking the "Catskill eagle in some souls." This bird, he states, "can alike dive down into the blackest gorges, and soar out of them again and become invisible in the sunny spaces. And even if he for ever flies within the gorge, that gorge is in the mountains; so that even in his lowest swoop the mountain eagle is still higher than other birds upon the plain, even though they soar." In other words, this majestic bird can, even in its deepest descents, in its darkest regions, still find higher worth than other flying creatures.

These are the lessons of Melville. Sadness reconciles us to realities. It throws us into the flow of life. It puts us on the brisk edge of experience. It makes the heart beat hard, throbbing between faith and doubt. Sadness says to the pining mind: it's fine to languish in incompleteness. It intones to the black mood: hold the darkness, for there in the somber closeness the brightest light will break. It sings to that early-morning hopelessness, caroling in a doleful refrain: stay in your bleakness; out of its blankness something will come, a new insight, a fresh way of seeing, of being.

Embracing our sighs and our languors, our solitudes and our meditations, we indeed gain painful insights otherwise hidden, novel knowledge of our selves and the world, original attitudes toward stale objects and ideas. We come to life and from that moment do not demonize melancholia. We no longer reduce sadness to weakness of will or sickness in need of a pill. We no more try to twist sadness into nothing but debilitating depression or manic hallucination. Instead, we dwell with those pensive moods that hope for something below the surface. We endure the incompleteness yearning for a vision of the whole. We seek the sorrowful joy.

MELVILLE WAS one of the first Americans to sound the somber and weird depths of the melancholy imagination. Doing so, he exemplified a largely hidden form of American genius. This kind of genius, closer to Europe than America, is largely Gothic, attuned as it is to dark things—to the desperate crows over the plains and to the lonely roads stretching into the gloom, to ruined barns, crepuscular and sinister, and to bones crumbling in the desert's afterglow. This sullen American genius shows up in the tormented canvases of Jackson Pollock and the nervous ebullience of Marilyn Monroe. It appears in the fevered confessions of Robert Lowell and the manic humor of Jim Carrey. It can be found in Sylvia Plath's haunted verse and Tom Waits's guttural laments. It shows up in the ruined faces of Edward Hopper and in Mark Rothko's blank squares.

I could list more great icons of American melancholia, dour counters to the bright visions of Bradford and Franklin (of Norman Rockwell and Norman Vincent Peale, of Anthony Robbins and Will Rogers). But I want to pause on one of the great moments in Gothic America, an instant that brings home with as much power as Melville the utter profundities that might emerge from melancholy meditation.

It was late December in 1981. In a house out in Colts Neck, New Jersey, a man entered a room containing a chair, an old guitar, a harmonica in a holder, and a simple four-track tape recorder. He picked up his guitar and then placed the harmonica holder on his neck. After a pause he put his lips on the harmonica and blew. Out came a piercingly lonesome sound, high and stark. This was a cry into the void—naked, helpless, and needy. This was the keen moan of mourning, a shrill dirge on all hopeless loss. There was no one there to listen. There was no heart open to the plaint.

This man was Bruce Springsteen, and the song into which he was heaving was "Nebraska," a song about a young murderer bleakly confessing his crimes. This was to be the first song on Springsteen's austere masterpiece, called *Nebraska*, after the title track. Through a soul-wrenching period, Springsteen wailed his sad anthems into his recorder. He sang of loners and outcasts, criminals and nomads, broken cops and men bent on believing something, anything, in this hard world. He described lost highways, ghostly refineries, and dead-end cities. Each song was raw, fevered, insomniac. Here was a primal and forlorn sermon against the pain of life.

Springsteen admitted that he was going through a melancholy mood during the time he recorded this album. He had just finished a highly public and successful tour in support of *The River*, an extreme commercial success. He was probably drained and dull, wondering if his music and his life were heading in the right direction. It was probably this sense of disorientation that led Springsteen some years later to seek out psychotherapy, a practice that would help him explore his sadness, not expunge it. As he later confessed, just after the release of *Devils & Dust* (2005), people with "something eating at them" are more interesting than those who are merely content.

Springsteen's *Nebraska* stands as a grim testament to the power of melancholia for plumbing the bewildering abysses of the human heart. Out of his sadness emerged a work of brilliance, an unforgettable instance of desperate beauty.

MELVILLE AND SPRINGSTEEN alert us to the energy of winter. We all know of this, the mind's winter. No leaves now hide the nakedness of the branches. We stare at the gnarled and exposed limbs. They shiver in the wind. The oak and the elm, the maple and the birch: all these formerly regal trees resemble poor souls desperate for clothing. But no one is around to hope for solace. All is blank. No one meanders through the lanes radiating affection. The trees simply stand there, alone. They are the failed rulers of a bleak land. Their domain is one of emptiness. Nothing stirs in the excruciating stillness. We have the feeling that there is room for almost anything to fill this wintry void. Something surely is going to happen out there in the vast spaces drained of all meaning.

Once we accept these seasons of mental winter as inevitable parts of our life—indeed, once we affirm them as essential elements of existence—then the paradox comes truly alive. We actually feel, in the midst of our sorrow, something akin to joy. I'm sure that we all have experienced this, that moment finally of giving over to our sadness, of not fighting it any longer. We then feel a strange vitality rise from the core of our very beings. We somewhere sense, probably deep in the unconscious, that we are now in our melancholia participating in life's vital fluxes, in the profoundest forces of the earth. We suddenly feel better—not blissfully happy but tragically joyful. We die into life.

The greatest tragedy is to live without tragedy. To hug happiness is to hate life. To love peace is to loathe the self. The blues are clues to the sublime. The embrace of gloom stokes the heart.

THE MAN OF SORROWS

Melancholy is sadness that has taken on lightness.
—ITALO CALVINO

AMERICAN HAPPINESS IS a temptation, one to which I've succumbed on several occasions. More than once I've grown weary of the pervasive gloom of my soul. Like millions of other Americans, I have tried to flee the sadness, attempted to escape, by any means possible, the weight, the fatigue, the fret. During these flights into shininess, I am rather sympathetic toward these American happy types. Let's be serious: life, in any form, is terribly and irredeemably hard. Why shouldn't we all scurry from the heartache in the most superficial ways possible, through BlackBerrys and Lexapro and liposuction? Why shouldn't we bask in the gaudy glow of the pervasive American dream? What's lost in this collective stupor? What's wrong, finally, with wanting nothing but bliss?

I know well what it's like to retreat into the tepid clichés of the collective, those armors defending us against the inevitable shocks of life. At the behest of well-meaning friends, I have purchased books on how to be happy. I have tried to turn my chronic scowl into a bright smile. I have attempted to become more active, to get out of my dark house and away from my somber books and participate in the world of meaningful action. I have taken up jogging, the Latin language, and the chair of a university English department. I have fostered the drive to succeed in my career. I have bought an insurance policy, a PalmPilot, and a cell phone. I have taken an interest in Thanksgiving and Christmas, in keeping my hair trimmed short, and in meticulously ironing my clothes. I have viewed Doris Day and Frank Capra movies. I have feigned interest in the health of others. I have dropped into the habit of saying "great" and "wonderful" as much as possible. I have pretended to take seriously certain good causes designed to make the world a better place. I have contemplated getting a dog. I have started eating salads. I have tried to discipline myself in nodding knowingly. I have tried to be mindful of others but ended up pissed as hell. I have written a book on the hard-earned optimism of Ralph Waldo Emerson. I have undertaken yoga. I have stopped yoga and gone into tai chi. I have thought of going to psychiatrists and getting some drugs. I have quit all of this and then started again and then once more quit. Now I plan to stay quit. The road to hell is paved with happy plans.

I must admit then that regardless of my own efforts to take flight through the many escapes America offers, my basic instinct is toward melancholia—a state I must nourish.

In fostering my essential nature, I'm trying to live according to what I see as my deep calling. Granted, it's difficult at times to hold hard to this vocation, this labor in the fields of sadness. But I realize somewhere in the core of my bones that I was born to the blues. If I don't adhere to this birthright, I would feel fake. My summons is to the mixed-up earth.

Surely some of you have felt the same way that I do. You have turned sullenly from those thousands of glowing, perfect teeth lighting the American landscape and slouched to the darkness—the half-lighted room, the twilight forest, the empty café. There you have sat and settled into the bare, hard fact that the world is terrible in its beauty, indifferent much of the time, incoherent and nervous and resplendent when on certain evenings, when the clouds are right, a furious owl swooshes luridly from the horizon. You feel that sweet pressure behind your eyes, as if you would at any minute explode into hot tears. You long to languish in this unnamed sadness, this vague sense that everything is precious because it is dying, because you can never hold it, because it exists for only an instant.

I remember this feeling from a very young age, and it has lived with me all my years: this feeling of nameless hopeful nostalgia. I suspect it has been with you as well. When I was a teenager, I longed most to spend my days, especially in summer, lolling about in my dark bedroom. With my blinds dimming the morning sun to a gloomy beam, I would lie on my floor and stare for hours at the stains on my ceiling: a handprint that blurred into a purplish root, a smudge from a dead bug resembling a star. I thought of nothing in particular but dissolved into the flitting shadows of my dissolute, nervous mind, now brooding over lost memories, now envisioning impossible futures. If there was any sort of persistent atmosphere to these vague images, it was a tremulous air of failure, a filmy focus on my broken heart among the fireflies or on those seven stitches from when I tumbled. The brisk chirp of a mockingbird outside my window enhanced this perverse joy, this decadence of embracing blackness while the world sprang into light. I loved my cold seclusion from song and flight, this winter of my mind's own making.

Around noon on each of those days, my dad threw open my door, raised my blinds, encouraged me to get out of bed. Go play baseball with the other boys, he suggested, or go swimming, or call a girl. Above all, he wanted me to be a red-blooded American boy, a go-getter, a fine young man. The sun's glare and his robust voice startled me every time. It was like being born again, thrown from the darkish and indiscriminate fluid onto a hot shore where everything is one thing and nothing else, where clocks clang and maps rule. I hated to have to move. But I always did.

I reluctantly adjusted to the demands of the daytime. I fitted myself into the white rules of the baseball diamond or used lucid sentences to convey thoughts. I killed reverie and endeavored to succeed. I pretended to be happy and forced myself to laugh. I took up saying "sir" and "ma'am." I mowed grass for money. I learned Bible verses at church in hopes of winning chintzy prizes. I feigned boredom with Tolkien and Frank Herbert and Salinger. I tried my best to make Bs and Cs on my tests, just so I could fit in with the other athletic mediocrities. But in spite of myself, I never did. My fervid mind always kicked in, and I reluctantly took my nerdy A. Then I returned for a time to my weird interiors—to the late Beatles and surreal poetry and Gregor Samsa.

I think that regardless of how happy we pretend to be, we have all undergone this struggle, this tension between our own dark feelings and the grating call of the bright, shiny, happy world. We grow weary of the guilt we feel over our melancholy souls. We want to be left alone so that we can brood for as long as we want. We want this because we feel most alive, most vital when we suffer this rich confusion over the things of the universe. We sense that we are with the world, its swift interplay of horrible and holy.

ONE CAN FLY from sadness. From sadness one can receive. The feeling of being thrown into a world not of our own making, the sense of being torn between equally appealing possibilities, the chronic anxiety over nothing in particular: if we don't flee from these seemingly inevitable situations, then we likely suspect that this sense of alienation, this on-going limbo, this relentless anxiety are calls for us to take responsibility for our own unique beings, for us to become, for once, authentic. We conclude that crisis is the crucible that burns away the inessential and reveals to us our vital core.

To sit long with our various alienations and our sumptuous paralyses and our nervous fears is to come indeed to a startling realization. It is this: melancholy connects us to our fundamental being. Think of it. If I am anxiously sad, I don't enjoy a comfortable relationship to the objects or people around me. They agitate me; they feel unfamiliar. I look around my house, for instance. I see my grocery list, my volumes of Proust, my television set, a picture of a friend. Each of these things is weirdly inaccessible. I wonder why I ever came by them, what they are doing in my house. I at one time might have thought that these were integral components of my life. Now, though, all of the sudden, they feel superfluous, as if they were seducing me away from what is most important. They become meaningless.

Unmoored from these familiar things, I am forced to look within myself, into my most mysterious interiors. Gazing within, I realize that I am ultimately alone in the world, that no one can live my life for me: not my wife, not my parents, not my culture. At this moment, when I am stripped of the familiar, I get in touch with what is most intimate: I am *this* person and no one else. I must find my unique potentialities, my own horizons. I must live my own life and die my own death. No one else can do this for me.

I am startled. I know: I am finite. I will die. My possibilities for living are limited. But at this very juncture when I feel most limited and most befuddled, I am granted a golden opportunity, a supreme invitation. I am called to imagine my own most idiosyncratic opportunities, my most personal potencies. I have only a brief time on this earth. I had better make the most of this time. Embracing my own death, I am shocked into living. Feeling my finitude, I envision infinite horizons for being.

This is a paradox. Existing with an eye toward death, I come to life. Feeling totally alone, I experience union with all of the living. Suffering inevitable anxiety, I undergo a vital shock. I get it: to be alive is to realize the universe's grand polarity. Life grows out of death, and death from life; turbulence breeds sweet patterns, and order dissolves into vibrant chaos. The cosmos is mixed, blurred, messy, and contradictory. But this mishmash keeps things jostling along, moving, unpredictable, contingent, mysterious, interesting. Suddenly my world doesn't feel as if I were endlessly channel surfing, clicking the button all night even though I've seen everything that flashes across my screen. On the contrary, I don't know what's coming next. I'm on my toes. I'm edgy, incomplete, and sad, but I'm trying to imagine poems more beautiful than the quiet cruising of devious sharks and symphonies more sonorous than those songs of the aloof birds of summer. I'm attempting to concoct a cosmos out of chaos.

I know these thoughts might sound morbid, but they're not meant to. Instead, these ideas are meant to be vital, exciting, liberating. Death in this light is not merely decay or rot or grave. It is a call to life, an electrical jolt enjoining us to explore, with vigor and wit, our own odds and risks. Death in this way proves an invitation to seize the day, to encounter the great theme of the carpe diem. As Robert Herrick, the seventeenth-century British poet, put it in his famous verse "To the Virgins, to Make Much of Time": "Gather ye rosebuds while ye may / Old Time is still a-flying; / And this same flower that smiles today / Tomorrow will be dying." In a less jocular vein, Walt Whitman, the nineteenth-century American poet, considers death in "Out of the Cradle Endlessly Rocking." In this poem, death is a "low and delicious word" whispered by the oscillatory ocean, a word that awakens in a young boy his capacity for gorgeous moonlight songs.

WITH HERRICK AND WHITMAN in my head, I venture out into the inhospitable world. The winter is indeed the time for walking alone through the cold muck and thinking of things unseemly to the masses. It is now the month of December. In the dawn's half-light I take a walk through my neighborhood. I can see my breath rise as smoke toward the whitish sky. The sun in the east is but a pale disk, sickly and barely discernible. I put my hands in my pockets and repress a shiver. I should be home in bed.

At the edge of the houses that I know, I happen upon an unexplored arbor of flaccid brown leaves, small reminders of the night's umber gloom. I take a step onto the damp ground. There is no crisp harvest crunch under my feet. There is only the dull press of wetness, soundless but for the occasional swish of slick sliding. I look down at these clammy leavings from the fall. Some are almost cinquefoil, reminding of dead hands.

But one of the leaves, I notice, seems not entirely expired.

It is a maple leaf retaining some of its autumnal purple. I slowly bend over to pick it up. It is cold in my bare hand. I stand up, holding its pomegranate-colored form. Its sheen of frost glistens like silver in the rising light. I get a quick chill and drop this gelid thing, three-pointed and close to dying. I continue my walk, now trying my hardest to see another living leaf, something orange this time, to recall to me the sweet Indian summer and warm my bones.

But then I find that someone else has been in this arbor before me. He has entered the grove with a rake and piled to one side a huge mound of leaves. They have been there for some time. They are soaked with old rain, and brown and rotting. I walk over to this lumpy half circle. Before I get within ten feet, I smell a horrible odor, a mixture of feces and death. The white winter sun now edges farther above the horizon and focuses its first tawdry beams directly onto this accumulation of refuse. I discover in this assortment of deceased leaves the severed plastic arm of some child's baby doll. It is dirty and mangled. I think of my own childhood toys, now probably blackening in some distant landfill. I turn away and begin the return to my house. I have lost my stomach for walking. I want to sit in a cream-colored room where nothing moves.

When I get back to my house, I find myself in my study. Something has happened to me, something that I must record. I strain to recapture my feeling of purple. It quickly comes, and there I am in my imagination weaving in and out of desolate trunks with my eyes wide open. In a flash of energy, I write several sentences on this experience. But then

rises in my mind that amassment of sludge and the doll fragment. I think to myself that I shouldn't be excited over this
season of sordid appendages and squalor. I stop writing. I
look over what I have written. It is turgid, hyperbolic. With
slight disdain, I begin to mark out extraneous words and
phrases. I feel the brisk satisfaction of making lean what had
before been bloated, of rubbing off a layer of dirt. In the end
I am left with three tight sentences and the slow-burning
rapture of successful creation, the play of energy and form,
the beating heart and the mind that's chilled.

I learn again that my lonely meditations on death breed
lively musings on life. I am further instructed in the mysteries of the universe, in the cosmic interplay between transience and permanence. Alerted to this pattern, I overcome
my alienation and realize that I, like all other creatures, am a
meeting place of wondrous oppositions, wings and dirt, stars
and slugs.

SUCH EXPERIENCES—and I've had more than one of
them—remind me constantly that there can really be no life
without death. This motif might seem foreign to most
Americans, but it really shouldn't. In this largely Christian
nation, many people, regardless of their claims to be happy,
are very close to this idea that the dark night of the soul con-
jures quick, undying light.

There is in the Christian tradition a picture of Jesus that
has little to do with happiness. Why Americans tend to

imagine Jesus as some sort of blissed-out savior, untroubled because divine, is beyond me. If we look closely at the four Gospels, we notice not a jovial minister but a tortured prophet, a man who realized from early on that the only way to gain salvation is to enter the deepest shadows.

Look at the career of Jesus. The man obviously struggled with his supposed dual nature, his division between god and human, spirit and matter. In his mind he could not be merely spirit, for then he would not be able to suffer the ills of death. Likewise, he could not be simply matter, because then he would lack the vision of the kingdom of heaven. He had to struggle between these two immense antagonisms and some-how bring them tenuously together.

Why else would he contend so intensely with his calling? Recall the night before he was to turn himself over to the Roman authorities, the powers that would surely crucify him. He retired to the Garden of Gethsemane to pray over his plight. There, among the foliage, he experienced keen anguish, so sharp that his sweat "was like drops of blood falling to the ground." Suffering this torment, he prayed all the harder. The nature of this prayer we do not know, though we can surmise that Jesus was invoking his God for clarity in the midst of confusion. I ground this supposition on what oc-curred later, when Jesus, undergoing the agony of crucifix-ion, wailed just before his death: "Father, Father, why hast thou forsaken me?" Only a man in terrible doubt would in-tone such a desperate query, one that questioned his entire sense of identity.

Most Christians for centuries have viewed Jesus as an otherworldly figure untouched by the troublous globe. An illuminated minority, however, has seen Jesus in another way, as a man of sorrows whose melancholy suffering was inseparable from his illumination. One member of this minority was Carl Jung, the great twentieth-century psychologist. In 1928, Jung received a strange document in the mail. The package came from Richard Wilhelm, an eminent Sinologist, and it contained an ancient Taoist alchemical treatise titled *The Secret of the Golden Flower.* Jung immediately found in this text parallels to some of his most cherished psychoanalytical ideas. But one notion in this old volume seemed especially resonant with Jung's own work: the sense that chaos is the original power of the universe, an indifferent reservoir out of which pairs of opposites arise. Jung had for years understood the value of this idea in his therapeutic work, realizing that seemingly separate oppositions are really interdependent manifestations of the same principle. For Jung, this principle was the unconscious, and out of this abyss emerged mutually inclusive oppositions, such as darkness and light, sadness and joy, female and male. In Jung's mind, this situation meant that melancholia and insight are intimately connected, that profound gloom generates rapid light, that dissolution is the key to transformation. With no loam, the glow holds no more.

Jung had reached these ideas earlier during his darkest period, a span running from 1913, when he underwent a traumatic break with his mentor Freud, to 1922, when he suffered the death of his mother. In the intervening years Jung experienced the terror of World War I, encountering horrific reveries and dreams of a "monstrous flood covering all the northern and low-lying lands between the North Sea and the Alps." When this flood reached Switzerland, his home country, it turned to "mighty yellow waves" on which floated the "rubble of civilization, and the drowned bodies of uncounted thousands." Then "the whole sea turned to blood." This vision left Jung, understandably, "perplexed and nauseated."

During this lengthy time of extreme melancholia, a period when Jung fell "into a state of disorientation," as though he were "totally suspended in mid-air," he came to realize this startling fact: neurosis—nervousness, agitation, unease—is essential in the shaping of identity. As he wrote in 1917, in the midst of his awful crisis, many people owe their "entire usefulness and reason for existence to neurosis," a power that prevents "critical follies" and forces one "to a mode of living" that develops "valuable potentialities." Neurosis is, after all, energy, a potent message sent from the unconscious. This missive informs an individual that he is out of balance, that he needs to alter his thoughts and actions if he is to return to health. In this way, neurosis is a catalyst for insight into the depths of the psyche, an inspiration to seek the interdependent opposite of ongoing dejection—not crass happiness but firm mental health, a balance between gloom and glee. Neurosis is knowledge.

Emerging from his own darkly neurotic period into a more vital state of mental health, Jung decided that he needed a place where he could retire to brood over the dynamic relationship between melancholia and meditation.

In 1922, just as his sad season ended, Jung bought some land in Bollingen, a small village located on the Lake of Zurich. There he began to build, by himself, a tower, a place of retreat. Once he completed the first section of this tower—he built three more sections over the years—he retired into its walls for hours. Dwelling in a tower with no electricity or running water, with no artificial heating or telephone, Jung sat alone and contemplated the relationship between psychic disintegration and mental wholeness.

It was likely in this tower that Jung first read *The Secret of the Golden Flower*, that ancient Taoist alchemical text. This book inspired him to begin his own researches into the alchemy of the Western world, a spiritual practice that had thrived during the Middle Ages and the Renaissance. Over the next several years Jung indeed realized that alchemy was not some greedy method for turning lead to gold. On the contrary, alchemy was a primitive form of psychoanalysis. As the alchemist watched lead burn down into a bubbling black chaos, he descended into the darkness of his own soul, that psychic place attuned to deathly melancholy. While he watched this substance cool down into a crust under the guidance of his various tinctures, he felt his own psyche emerge from the gloom into the partial light, into the twilight or the dawn. Then, finally, after he had added yet other tinctures, he witnessed this crust turn into a reddish gold. Watching this occur, he experienced a rise in his own soul, an ascent from shadows to full light, a move from the moon to the sun. Yet the alchemist always understood this bracing condition: the sun is but preparation for another night. To gain even deeper knowledge of his interior, he would again have to break down his substance and his soul and once more suffer the sinister knowing of the heart's dark night.

Jung's alchemical studies ultimately led him to a new comprehension of the Christ. He believed that the life of Jesus was ultimately a parable for the alchemical process and thus, in turn, for the psychic process by which one moves from necessary melancholy to a grasp of the essential self. Seen in this light, Jesus during his crucifixion was beset by dark confusion, a bewildering and painful disintegration of the old self, the material self. This dissolution, this rending, was preparation for a new resolution, a fresh wholeness. After three days in the tomb, a threshold space, Jesus—as it says in the myth—enjoyed transformation into a new being. But according to the alchemical tradition on which Jung drew, this new Jesus was not some unworldly deity but a mixture, polarized, a melding of darkness and light, female and male, anti-Christ and Christ. In other words, the risen Christ was a *self*, a site of dynamic, interdependent opposites.

I often wonder if America would be better off, would be a richer and deeper nation, if it took seriously Jung's version of Jesus. Then we would no longer flock to the optimistic Christianity of Norman Vincent Peale or Billy Graham. Though Peale published *The Power of Positive Thinking* in 1952, his saccharine version of Christianity still persists today. Peale's plan for success is a typically American melding of capitalism and Christianity. His technique for eliminating all negative feelings from life is to intone a series of positive sayings, what we would now call affirmations. Mumbling these mantras daily will lead, Peale promises, to a successful life, a life in which all dreams, American and otherwise, come true. The key is to repeat these sayings until they sink into the unconscious and secretly organize our lives. For instance, one can repeatedly whisper to oneself, at least ten times a day, one of Peale's own affirmations: "I expect the best and with God's help will attain the best." When we murmur this or another like expression enough times, then we shall, according to Peale, become vessels of the divine, a power that wants nothing more than for us to succeed—to gain comfort in this world. What is Jesus in this paradigm but an accomplished man of the world?

On June 12, 1966, Billy Graham, in a sermon to the National Council of Churches, claimed that no one had "done more for the kingdom of God than Norman and Ruth Peale." On one level, this is a strange proclamation, since Graham has a keen sense of sin and makes guilt a main component of his theology. But on another level, his praise of Peale isn't that surprising. Like Peale, Graham believes that Jesus is a heal-all, a sort of simpleminded therapist capable of brushing away major maladies like depression in the blink of an eye. For instance, on his website, billygraham.org, Graham attempts to minister to a depressed woman who has written him a letter wondering if God really cares about her. Graham advises that this woman try not to focus on her pain but instead key her attention to "Christ." Through directing her energy toward the supposed love of this ostensibly resurrected savior, she will quickly feel healing powers afoot and soon will be released from her sadness. "Pray," Graham writes, "and the promises of

God's Word can do much to keep those [negative] feelings at bay." This message is one constantly purveyed in one of Graham's recent books, *Hope for the Troubled Heart: Finding God in the Midst of Pain* (1991). Graham argues that sorrow is a result of sin and that proper prayer to God will ultimately help us overcome our sadness.

If we in America could avoid these versions of Jesus, then we might move, slowly and with caution, to the more melancholy European portraits of Jesus. We would spend hours gazing at Matthias Grünewald's *The Crucifixion*, from around 1515. This German painting of Jesus depicts an emaciated man nailed to a simple wooden cross. He writhes in agony. One stark spike impales his two feet to the hard pole. Blood drips from his clenched toes. His stretched skin is covered in crimson droplets. So unbearable is the torture that the man's hands are trying to rip themselves free from the nails. But his face, defeated, downcast, crowned in thorns, ensures that he will not succeed. He is lonely, alienated, forsaken. Nothing can ease this anguish. Nothing can persuade us that this figure is anything more than a man suffering the worst dolor imaginable: to be confused and alone and close to dying.

Or perhaps we would over the course of a day peruse *The Dark Night of the Soul* of St. John of the Cross, also from the sixteenth century. St. John, a Spanish monk, explores the great melancholia one must endure in finding his way to a mysterious God. He holds up Christ as a paragon of the gloomy purgation of the senses, as a man who blinded his eyes to the superficial things of the universe and focused his inner sight on the lucid darkness of God. John's Jesus is a man used to dark chambers and dim forests. He lurks in corners and behind shadows. He is seeking something among the umbrageous bodies, something those hungry only for light are too weak and wanton to see.

Or we might, if we were avoiding Peale and Graham and their visions of a euphoric Jesus, choose a more recent rendering of Christ as the man of sorrows: Salvador Dalí's *Christ of St. John of the Cross*, from the middle of the twentieth century. This weird depiction, inspired by St. John of the Cross, shows Jesus from above, covered in shadows. The tormented savior looks down from the shade into a strange sky filled with reddish clouds, below which are a lake and a boat at the ready. This Christ, hovering in the darkness, is divorced from the light and from the liberating vessel below. He is entrapped in atmospheric blackness.

BILLY GRAHAM and Norman Vincent Peale are ministers for the suburbs. This really means that they are preachers for almost all of America, a country quickly becoming a vast suburb. What could be a greater sign that we as a country are largely relinquishing our creative unease, our desire to question a world that doesn't seem quite right? Think about suburban life. Out in the gated community, one rarely has to face the hard realities of the city. The suburban existence is an exit plan. This mode of living puts people out of the fray. There behind the predictable sheens they are safe from harm.

Gated communities have indeed become the new suburbia. With iron or stone walls surrounding hundreds of acres of formerly good forests, these self-contained communities are sequestered from the gorgeous turmoil of the organic world. In almost all these communities, one finds, after passing security, uniform one-acre plots surrounding a handful of stereotypical architectural styles: Tudors, Cape Cods, châteaux, and Italian villas. These houses likely came from a catalog of prefabricated plans. Many of these communities contain their own amenities—franchised stores, shops, restaurants. One need not ever leave the comfortable fold, unless one drives one's SUV into town to work a job or to purchase specialty items. What does this new trend signify but an increasing unwillingness to live in the world as it really is: unpredictable, unrepeatable, heterogeneous? We have forsaken the concrete for the contented.

Suburbia, a flight from the real, has become, even more recently, a virus. Having spread to take over almost all available marshlands and forests, suburbanization now must move inward. It's steadily flowing back into the cities. Take, for instance, Times Square. As late as the eighties and early nineties Times Square was a seedy synecdoche of all that was glorious and grimy about New York City. One could around Forty-second Street encounter a seductive mixture of divas and drugs, gloriously dilapidated buildings and grim rings of illegal sex. Now, after the infiltration of a Disney store in the middle of the square, the place feels little different from a family-friendly amusement park. In the wake of the Disney invasion, other benign franchises quickly followed. Times Square (though admittedly safer) soon lost its unique identity, and it became just another plot on which prefabricated buildings and businesses were placed. Before long it had the drab predictability of a suburban mall.

The new Time Warner Center in New York City is a horrendous example of this trend, this transformation of American cities into suburban malls. The buildings composing this conglomeration are made entirely of glass. Like the exteriors of most shopping malls, these structures, immense silver boxes, have no unique expression to speak of. They are smooth and blank, bland and blinding. But they are not aberrant. On the contrary, these kinds of glass buildings are increasingly the norm in our cityscapes. Towering metallic mirrors, signs of pervasive paranoia, set their glare throughout our blocks. No longer do we see the fading grandeur of nineteenth-century architecture, those expressive textures and vivid colors. No longer do we see matter, opaque and solid.

Few inhabiting these gated communities and the urban malls likely give a thought to the environmental costs of these postmodern conveniences. The more we are told that our natural resources are finite, the more we move in droves to the forests and the deserts and the more we dwell in glass buildings that require huge quantities of heating and air conditioning. Why on earth do we do the exact opposite of what we should be doing? We are in love not with actual atmospheres but with abstract predictabilities—with security over sanctification, with smooth monotones over pied poplars.

This love—if one can call it that (it's more like appetite)—of bland comfort will one day ironically get us exactly what we think we want, an utterly undifferentiated wasteland where everything is exactly the same as everything else, a razed plain of sand or ice, the logical extreme of this transformation of thriving ecosystems into sleek malls. This is a high price to pay for superficial bliss. We trade glistening leaves for peevish shimmering.

Can I really blame the happy types for our country's obsession with the mall mentality? Surely I can't. But I can point to the coincidence. I can notice that happy types want to boil the world down to quick contentment. I can note that these same happy types favor bland easiness over the hustled jostling of city life or wilderness. What other conclusion do I want to draw? Happy people reduce the earth to a series of glittering boxes. They make it the mirror of their muted souls.

We melancholy souls no doubt keenly feel the loss of our great old cityscapes and our forests and marshes. We love the beautiful ruins of aged buildings. We love the intricate architectural designs, the carvings and the mosaics and the rough stones. We love high ceilings and crown moldings. We love worn-down hardwood floors. We love the smell of rusting radiators. We love rickety windows that rattle in the wind. We also adore those ancient and lovely woodlands where we can walk alone and hear geese honking over the horizon. We can't get enough of trees in winter, of the thin brownish pines wisping among the oaks that never move. We are mad about the mucky earth covered in dead leaves. We inhale the nostalgic air and feel alive.

Our melancholy sense of impending death, of coming ruins and trunks that totter, gives us a special appreciation of each thing's unique being. We think: here, right here, this particular being exists in its own way and will soon die its own death. We are sad for the going but exhilarated over the sudden eruption of beauty rising from the decrepitude. The run-down building, the fading elm: these burn their brightest before they yield over to inexorable time and die. They are not gentle in their rage against the night. We stand in awe as these beings explode into an ecstasy of somber light.

I live in a house built in 1920. Its bricks are beginning to crumble away, and its roof needs work. The furnace in the basement is big and brown and lumbering and often in need of repair. The house's floors are worn and stained. The windows in winter barely resist the blasts of freezing air. The place is frigid most of the time, even in summer. A gnarled old maple tree rests in my front yard. It looks cranky and unsuited for photographs. I love this old wreck of a building. I'd never trade it in for one of those warm and efficient prefabricated houses in the suburbs. I enjoy its sweet decadence too much. When I come home from melancholy walks in my neighborhood—near the city and the oldest in town—I love to stand in front of my decomposing abode. In the twilight, the face of my house and the tree in front of it stand alone in the world. There is nothing to match them. They are rotting. They are more beautiful than the noon sun.

———————

THE MAIN PROBLEM WITH this mall mentality is that it grows out of an obsession with abstraction. Obviously, one can't even begin to think or speak without using abstractions such as "red" or "dog" or "human" or whatnot—general terms that subsume several particular examples: that vermilion tint at twelve o'clock during the summer; a German shepherd running with its back toward a birch; that woman combing her hair as she broods in the winter night. However, if one becomes overly enamored of abstractions, one ultimately forgets the concrete world from which the abstractions rose in the first place. One reduces all the different events of the world to the same concept. One no longer perceives a particular vermilion but only the idea of redness. One no more experiences that specific wag of the tail but the notion of "dogness." And one doesn't anymore see those unrepeatable follicles but the grid "womanness."

If one possesses the mall mentality—and with it a penchant for prefabricated architecture of any kind, including, especially, the brick boxes of gated communities—then one favors the same over the different. Malls, wherever one goes, are basically the same. Gated communities, in whatever region, are also basically one. To spend one's time in malls of all kinds or around imprisoning housing communities, one comes after a while to forget or ignore or repress the concrete environments over which these monotonous structures have been built. That particular cityscape—Times Square, for instance—is lost in favor of a generalized Disney store, one of thousands nationwide. That specific forest—a unique ecosystem—is forsaken for a community blueprint used in developments throughout the country. In both instances, one loses an immediate experience of what's most alive in this world, the exquisite "thisness." In the name of comfort and predictability, in the name of American happiness, one comes to love ghostly ideas and wispy notions, moribund haunts and filmy grids.

No one was more attuned to the glories of the particular and the dangers of the general than William Blake. When Blake (whom we have already met, however briefly) was but a boy, he walked through the hayfields surrounding old London. One day he saw above the grain angels spangling the branches of a tree. His mother beat him for recounting this vision. Later, as an adult running his own printing shop, he regularly conversed with angels about his art. His contemporaries, unsurprisingly, feared he was losing his mind. These contrasts between Blake's visions of spirits and the societal censuring that followed could only lead him to conclude that his reasonable culture was in conspiracy against the spiritual life. No wonder this fervidly creative man was endlessly beset by what he called "nervous fear." He was being persecuted at the stern bar of abstraction, a system of laws that requires everyone to see exactly the same thing—not that tree brimming with wings but a staid oak.

Blake turned his dream-fueled dread into attacks on the priests, kings, and thinkers reducing the world to reason. For Blake, flattening experience to comfortable predictability is akin to fitting the capacious cosmos into ratios, grids based on lowest common denominators. The sun, says common sense, can only be a disk hanging in the sky. To see it as a fiery ball of angels intoning holy songs is to risk being labeled mad.

Transforming his anxious melancholia into a palpable sense of particulars, Blake, in his 1798 marginalia to the works of a famous artist of his time, Sir Joshua Reynolds, proclaimed that "To Generalize is to be an Idiot. To Particularize is Alone Distinction of Merit." "General Knowledge" does not exist, while "Singular & Particular Detail is the Foundation of the Sublime." These distinctions reverse traditional expectations. Ideas, generally the essentials of knowledge, become delusions. Immediate perceptions, flashes usually corralled into concepts, are now revelations of the real. Theories are ignoble reductions. Direct apprehensions open into the infinite.

Blake believes that the sublime arises from a sensual scrutiny so intense that it penetrates to an unbounded energy at the heart of distinct forms. As he intones in *The Marriage of Heaven and Hell* (1793), "If the doors of perception were cleansed every thing would appear to man as it is: infinite." This cleansing requires enhanced sensation: "the whole creation will appear infinite" only through "an improvement of sensual enjoyment." Favoring the abstract over the concrete, one "sees all things only thro' the narrow chinks of his cavern." Practicing immediate perception, one apprehends infinity in a grain of sand, and in a bird, an unseen world of delight.

How does abstraction, seemingly attuned to spirit, lead

to narrowness and illusion? How does intense perception, ostensibly shackled to matter, open to infinity, to eternity? For Blake, abstraction is egocentric and retrospective. One's concepts, no matter how putatively universal, arise from past personal experiences. My conception of my ego is an abstraction extrapolated from a selection of past experiences that arrange themselves into a consistent narrative. My ideas of love and blueness and black cat and whatnot are ghostly précis arising from numerous particulars of my past, mostly forgotten. These memorial abstractions are necessary for negotiations of experience. However, if one believes that the retrospective ego and its abstractions are the only realities, then one reduces the present to a cipher of the past. He flattens the world to a double of his interior archives. He is doomed to undergo the same experiences over and over. He turns and turns and turns in what Blake calls the "same dull round."

Intense perception is charitable and prospective. If one breaks through egocentric, retrospective abstractions and immediately apprehends a particular moment, then one does not encounter an example of one's past, a reduction of the world to the ego's double. He experiences the concrete event as a discrete, unique pattern of a transpersonal, ungraspable energy. Scrutinizing this thing here, now—his beloved or a crocus—he moves from self-consciousness to other-consciousness. He becomes entranced by this particular "isness." He gazes with increasing intensity. Suddenly he senses in this entity naked existence, the mystery of being. The thing becomes an event, a confluence of form and energy, other and same. This vision is of eternity in time.

But what is eternity? It is not unending duration, time everlasting. It is the pure present, not bound to memory and fraught with nostalgia or regret and not bound to foresight and vexed with fear or anticipation. Not troubled by the pressures of history, eternity is not tensed, not tied to finite verbs. It is infinite. Infinite does not mean boundlessly large, space unceasing. Infinity is pure presence, beyond comparison with other presences that have surrounded and will surround, beyond environmental limitation. Transcending temporal and spatial distinctions, eternity and infinity— negations of the abstractions of minutes and points—are openings into a realm in which before and after, here and there blur into a hum of ungraspable being.

This recondite language (ironically abstract) can be viewed in a concrete context. Blake in his annotations to Lavatar's *Aphorisms on Man* (1788) says: "the Philosophy of Causes & Consequences misled Lavatar as it has all his contemporaries. Each thing is its own cause & its own effect[.] Accident is the omission of act in self & the hindering of act in another. This is Vice but all Act . . . is Virtue. To hinder another is not an act it is the contrary it is a restraint on action both in ourselves & in the person hinderd." To expect people and things to conform to a determining past and a determined future, to a limiting environment and a bounded horizon, is to hinder them, to impose upon them grids that deprive them of ineffable impulses and unexpected swerves. If one sees only those characteristics that conform to these abstractions, then he commits vice, the reduction of self and other to stable units forever divided: cause and effect, subject and object. In contrast, if one can break through abstractions and perceive immediately another person or thing, then one experiences a being that is the effects of its own causes, free of past and future, context and horizon. To see a being in this way—as an unrepeatable revelation of eternity and infinity— is to enjoy virtue: the unwillingness to thwart the irreducible otherness of *that* or *this*; the willingness to open to how the event uniquely torques the abiding, though unknowable, pressure of being.

If Blake had been attuned only to contentment, then he would have settled for those lowest common denominators of experience, those ratios that flatten specific to general. But this man, stoked on his turbid melancholia, was never comfortable with the status quo. He wanted to see through the stern networks of his culture to the teeming world beyond. There he saw not mere mud and mire but pulses of indomitable brightness. Of course Blake and his fellow melancholics—I include myself in this group—are not entirely free from abstractions. However, they at least desire to break through mental barriers (Blake elsewhere calls them "mind-forg'd manacles") to something unique and living: flashing apples at dawn, contorted roots under the moon.

IT'S FINALLY the smoothness that kills us. Happy types around the country seem bent on ironing out all the rough edges, not only those cragged corners of old houses and those weather-weary knots on old oaks but also the wrinkled faces born of strain and the gravelly tops of lonely and decrepit highways. Our world is quickly becoming nothing but a glazed sphere, uniform as glass. Mountains will soon be flattened, and valleys made level. The planet will soon turn into an immense marble garishly floating through the dark spaces, alien as shadows, and among the stars, forlorn and alone, that flash their prickled light.

Some of you probably remember the weirdness of long road trips. You loaded up in a rumbling old sedan. Once you left the precincts of your town you quickly found yourself on an old highway. The pavement was everywhere cracked and frequently pocked with potholes. As you jostled over the uneven surface, you didn't think about grading the asphalt with fresh blacktop. Instead, you were mesmerized by those leaning and crazed-looking establishments on the road's shoulder. You wondered what on earth could be in those buildings with chipping paint and rusty doors. You at least knew that it would be a little dark inside and that you would probably smell old burlap sacks and the faint odor of tar. You could definitely get some strange-shaped rock candy and maybe some cold chocolate milk. Behind the counter was probably a shadowy man smelling of wintergreen. Beyond those probable things, you had no idea what was inside that gas station or that tourist shop or that diner. You might find anything—pig's feet or painted chicks or the skulls of cows or bullwhips or tough jerky or comics from forgotten wars or posters of Roy Rogers or a dried-up bat. You might recoil from these strange elements, but you would never forget them, not in a lifetime. You would also recall the melancholy atmospheres of those places, redolent of musty decay.

Now going on a road trip is a much different experience. You slide into a sleek new foreign car and in minutes reach the interstate highway. The road is smooth as silk; you feel almost as though you were riding on untroubled air. There is nothing to break the monotony along the way but bland green exit signs pointing to the obvious eateries—McDonald's or Subway or Taco Bell—or the expected convenience marts— Shell or Exxon or Amoco. You pull off to grab a bite or fill your tank. You realize that this exit is exactly like every other exit around the country. Everything is the same—safe, clean, predictable. This is smooth travel, flat as a stainless steel iron.

The same is true of faces these days; they're as unblemished as flat plastic. You probably increasingly long for those world-worn gazes, crisscrossed with strain. You realize the beauty of those countenances that have pressed against the oncoming years, that have suffered honestly the abrasions and contusions of life. These expressions are manifestations of unmentionable inner struggles, of riddling nights spent alone poring over yellowing books, of beautiful days, dosed on crocus, lost forever. Inscribed on these visages are mysteries endlessly engaging, curious runes worthy of long study. You could stare at these faces as you would a work of art, a Miró or an Escher. In your study of these cragged physiognomies, you would discern perhaps a lifetime, a whole personal history. You would say to yourself: This person *is*. She suffered, and she learned.

But what do we say about those ubiquitous guises of our contemporary scene, those appearances Botoxed to the max? You catch these smooth and expressionless faces when you walk down a city street. You can find no trace of existence in these frozen masks. You sense that these people have been utterly happy and totally well adjusted for their entire lives. These almost metallic appearances seem to have known no strife. You don't want to stare too long at these overly finished exteriors; you might be blinded by the glare. Or worse, you might actually see this person for what he is—a husk, nothing but an unfilled form. Then you would fear the worst. Our world is teeming with these phantom creatures, these zombielike beings. This is the postmodern horror show.

We've had enough of sanders and shiners, of those who would make our ragged, rough world smooth all over. We want to lose ourselves in the mottled mixes of the botched cosmos. We want for hours to gaze at an old face in a black-and-white photo, one of those ancient pictures found in an attic and stained with rain. We wish to sit by the grizzled highway—oaks, hoary and twisted, hover at our backs—and dream of deserts broken only by bones. We finally desire to stay up very late one night and on a whim walk to the bathroom mirror. There in the glass we witness our own expression. It is, we must conclude, rather sad and worn. We smile broadly and quickly recoil. We slowly return to our normal look and find, in our heartbroken eyes, beauty.

GENERATIVE MELANCHOLIA

Depression opens the door to beauty of some kind.
—JAMES HILLMAN

IN THE TWILIGHT of the fifteenth century, on an evening on which the Florentine sun radiated a crimson glow, sepulchral and lurid, Marsilio Ficino, the aging philosopher of Cosimo de' Medici's court, found himself once more in a woeful mood. Born under the sign of Saturn, the most sullen of planets, Ficino had suffered such sorrowful periods for as long as he could remember. Almost from his beginning—he was born in 1433, when the dolorous planet was ascendant—Ficino had struggled with his tendency to fall into fits of sighing and lassitude, pessimism and gloom. Now, as he was approaching the final years of his life, he was growing somewhat weary of the emotional turbulence. He wondered if he could, during the portentous season before his demise, find a way to interpret his chronic melancholia in a positive light, if he could salvage some solace from his overly pensive condition. He wanted to discover mirth in the murkiness.

In the past Ficino had often attempted to escape his melancholy periods by throwing himself into his work. He was a scholar of Greek and Latin and a thinker of the first order. Whenever Cosimo could purchase a rare text from the ancient Greek world, the powerful statesman commissioned his most distinguished philosopher to translate the work into Latin. For most of his adult life Ficino translated and wrote commentaries on the works of Plato. Such labor often soothed his heart and took his mind away from his nervous fears. But as he reached his sixtieth year, Ficino was growing tired of this escapism. He wanted to accept his melancholy disposition. He wished to embrace this agitation even though his learning in ancient and medieval medicine had taught him this: the melancholy constitution is probably the worst condition a person can suffer.

Ever since the fifth century B.C., people had feared the most sinister of the four humors: melancholia, or black bile. In classical Greece, physicians like Hippocrates believed that the body was composed of four humors. These were cholera, phlegm, blood, and, of course, melancholia. According to the ancient theory, these humors dictated dispositions. A chronically irascible man suffered from too much cholera. A tranquil individual possessed an overload of phlegm. A vigorous soul enjoyed a good quantity of blood. And a morose person was beset by a predominance of black bile.

This melancholy person was open to the most pernicious evils. He could turn misanthropic, fearful, despondent, nervous, or mad. In the words of Galen, a Hippocratic physician from late antiquity, melancholics "hate everyone whom they see, are constantly sullen and appear terrified, like children or uneducated adults in deepest darkness."

This tradition of negative melancholy continued in the European Middle Ages. In the works of pious thinkers like Hildegard of Bingen, black bile was excoriated as the cause of a troubling litany of sins. These sins included lust, sloth, and greed. Medieval psychologists believed that this combination of sins turned the melancholic into a reclusive voyeur, a lonesome hoarder. This wretchedly solitary life made him especially susceptible to demonic possession and blasphemous despair.

Physicians in the ancient world and the Middle Ages alike treated this seemingly terrible disease with an array of painful cures. The primary remedy involved bloodletting. Doctors believed that leeches and other methods of draining blood might remove the excess of black bile. Another cure based on the same idea was purgation. The favored purgative for melancholia was black hellebore. This herb was believed to have grown initially from the tears of a little girl who had no gift for the Christ child. Imbibing this wistful flower, the patient actually tried to transform his melancholia into disposable waste. There were yet other cures during these times. One involved hot baths meant to counter the coldness of melancholy. Another entailed overexposures to moisture; it was thought that the abundant water could overturn the dryness of the gloomy disposition.

The point of all these remedies is clear. Melancholia was

a vile disease that should be treated like the gout or fever, regardless of the pain of the cure. The best one could do for this disease was to remove it from the system.

Such visions of melancholy have of course persisted for centuries and have inspired numerous humiliating cures. In the eighteenth century, people beset with too much spleen, the period's term for black bile, were made to undergo rigorous regimens of exercise as well as potentially purgative sessions with the hypnotist. During the nineteenth century, doctors prescribed opium and laudanum to quell the mood of overmuch woe. Doing so, these physicians threw thousands upon thousands of melancholy souls into a terrible addiction, one that dulled the mind and wrenched the body. Such negative views of melancholy have recently grown to mammoth proportions. Our contemporary American culture has rather unwittingly taken these older views deeply to heart, turning violently on melancholia as if it were a terrible disease. With our many pharmaceuticals designed to fight sadness, we might destroy dejection completely. We might finish the work that began all those years ago, in the ancient world of humors and leeching. We might well leave on the earth nothing but sapless happiness.

Long before our American obsession with removing sorrow from the marrow, Ficino, as I have said, wished to counter Western history's prevailingly negative view of the mood. He wanted to find a positive way to interpret melancholy. Deep down he sensed that sadness was something much more than disease or sin. In fact, he had an inkling that the gloomy disposition might be especially well suited to the philosophical mood, perhaps even to intellectual brilliance. But where was he to find support for this hypothesis? In what authoritative text would he discover a friend to his melancholy soul, a guide through the dark and labyrinthine forest to the bright green field?

FICINO FOUND ready aid in a Greek text that came his way through the good offices of Cosimo. This text featured an ancient work titled *Problems*, possibly written by Aristotle himself. Embedded in this book was the following passage: "Why is it that all those who have become eminent in philosophy or politics or poetry or the arts are clearly melancholics?"

Brooding over this passage, Ficino saw the light within the darkness. He realized that his melancholy constitution need not be anathema at all. He understood indeed that his sad moods could be seen as virtues. Melancholia, he grasped, is far from a sickness. It is essential for the thinker's mental health, a sign of intellectual grace.

Moved by this query, Ficino set about writing one of his last books, *The Book of Life* (1489). This is a powerful treatise on the integral relationship between melancholy and meditation. In this groundbreaking book, Ficino countered the prevailing negative views of melancholy. He argued that the blues can be the catalyst for a special kind of genius, a genius for exploring dark boundaries between opposites.

According to Ficino, melancholy is most likely to afflict profound philosophers. These philosophical souls are dissatisfied with what passes for knowledge in the outside world, the rather banal realm of the status quo. Disorientated when they are out in the glare of the workaday world, these meditative sorts spend hours alone. They walk by themselves in the thick forest where the sun never shines. They sit alone at the corner table even while the crowds around them guffaw at the least thing. In their long solitude they brood hard on their interiors, those secret places within that no one but they can see. They attempt to penetrate to the very centers of their beings. They want to understand what exists at their very core. They hope that their apprehension of this rich and complex place will translate to a comprehension of the earth's innermost truth. They believe—these melancholy thinkers—that their deepest self is one with the immense cosmos.

Exploring connections between inside and outside, the sorrowful intellectual becomes an adept at a special kind of knowledge: he grows into an expert on boundaries, thresholds, borderlines. Most people migrate to one side of the world or the other. Some embrace their inner worlds and ignore the outside, with its moist, lubricious flows and its quick, coruscating patterns. Others focus on the world outside and repress their inner energies, those endless streams of surprising ideas and those concepts as stable as the fixed stars. Choosing one side or the other, these people live only half-lives. They tend to become heads without bodies or mere materials with no sense of soul. They take this route because it makes life easy, conclusive. They can say, with almost blind conviction, that their side is superior and the other side is meaningless. The Christian fundamentalist, valuing what he calls spirit over matter, can comfortably attack all those who value this earth's quick and dead. The secular hedonist, valorizing body over the notion of soul, can likewise with seeming impunity challenge those misty-eyed idealists. Both groups—and there are many analogous ones—divide the world to conquer it.

Melancholy philosophers, as Ficino describes them, avoid this rather easy and simple taking of sides. Knowing that truth is likely to thrive in the middle ground, between oppositions—between inside and outside, contemplation and action, unseen and seen—sorrowful thinkers delve into the crepuscular continuum between clarity and clarity. They think that edges, circumferences, and fringes are the most interesting places in the world, for there on the terminals things reveal their deepest mysteries: their blurred identities, their relationships to opposites, their tortured duplicities. Choosing to hover in this limbo between traditional oppositions, sorrowful thinkers feel themselves pulled asunder. On the one hand, they are committed to the world of soul, the invisible realm attuned to eternity. On the other hand, they are prone to the spectrum of bodies, the visible region controlled by time. Quivering on the interstices between these two areas—between metaphysical, one might say, and physical—these sad philosophers become strange mixtures, half souls and partial bodies. But this mix between oppositions reveals the rich mysteries of each pole. On the boundary between soul and body, one learns how those two antinomies differ and how they are the same, how their edges are shaped and how their centers pulse, how they are duplicitous and also whole.

Now, here, almost in the middle of this book, we find the deep heart of melancholia, its perseverance and its power. In pushing thinkers into the confused middle between two extremes, in forcing a journey into fertile limbo, melancholia invites a vision of a healing third term, a golden mean, a synthetic element that somehow reconciles, however tenuously, the antagonisms that appear to rip the universe asunder. If moody meditators could only discover this healing idea, then they could apprehend and reveal the interdependence between oppositions, the great secret of polarity. No more would the cosmos be torn in two; no more would viciously contentious antinomies be diametrically aligned. Suddenly, quick and coveted concord would flash into sight. The profound depths of the heart would mesh with the boundless heights of the heavens. The most abstract theories would find their substance in concrete actions. Intuitions would discover blood. Invisible potencies would actualize in the palpable. A secret relationship between these opposites, a dynamic ground of "both/and," would emerge. Sensing this concord, we would enjoy a profoundly tense peace, a sinister shining.

This, at least, is Ficino's hope: that the melancholy philosopher, after a long season of brooding on the boundary between conflicting potencies, will discover a hidden complicity, an untapped concord. This sudden harmony suggests that body and soul, sensation and feeling, brain and consciousness are not mutually exclusive oppositions, not occurrences forever at odds. On the contrary, this sudden insight into secret marriages between antinomies intimates that body takes form through the offices of soul and that the soul finds expression through the motions of the body. In the same way, the way we physically experience the world is informed by how we feel about this same world, and the manner in which we discover our moods is organized by the disposition of our anatomy. Likewise, our neurons generate our consciousness; our minds inform our synapses. In each case—in each instant that we understand these connections between opposites—we grasp not simple unity, that flaccid contentment sought by happy types. We apprehend a dynamic concord, an agitated mixture from which emerges a tenuous solution. We sense a patterned turbulence, a chaotic synthesis.

YOU ARE WITNESSING the birth of a child. The labor you see is extreme. The mother strains against the agony. She is in the final stages, only seconds away from pressing through her canal a living form. She gives her body another screaming heave. The top of a head emerges, purple and convex. Another wail produces another push. More of the head pushes out. Then a final thrust of the abdomen, more powerful than a planet, squeezes out a full face. The eyes are as distant as dull stars. They yearn already to return to the quiet darkness and are bewildered by the whirling light and sound. But it's too late. The tiny body quickly follows the head. A baby appears. You who have been watching are torn between weeping and laughing. You lament this infant's tragic fall into the pain of time; you celebrate this burst of new life. While the baby cries in lamentation and celebration, you join it, with your tears washing over your ridiculous grin. You at this moment are two and one at once, melancholy and joyful, sorrowful and ebullient. You realize that the richest moments in life are these junctures where we realize, in our sinews, what is true all the time: the cosmos is a dance of joggled opposites, a jolted waltz.

You are at a marriage. All wait tensely as the minister interrogates the man and the woman, asking them if they are really committed one to the other. Finally, this robed official reaches the end of his inquiries. He is on the verge of pronouncing this couple chronically bound. You notice that almost everyone around you is silently crying. Even the man and the woman quivering before the minister have glistening eyes. As the minister proclaims that two are made one, you feel yourself likewise begin to cry. You are happy and yet sad. Once more you realize in your heart of hearts that this is life at its deepest and richest, a moment when tragedy and comedy achieve a spirited mix, when the world's sorrow—these two in front of you must relinquish their egos to each other—and the world's joy—these two before you will never again have to be alone—come hesitantly together. Feeling this mixture of strife (these two egos will inevitably clash) and harmony (these two egos will probably reconcile), you are at once depressed and elated, ultimately exhilarated by the mystery of marriage, a wrenching paradox in which two hearts are ripped from their familiar contexts and crammed somehow into one unit.

You are at a funeral. This occasion celebrates a person

tepidly loved, a person as good as he was bad. Still, the people in the pews seem sad. They are bereft of yet another acquaintance. One more man is ready to sink back into the cold earth. You are likewise dolorous, even though you didn't know this person very well at all. You are disconsolate mainly over death itself, over the fact that you too will soon join this man in the planet's inhospitable dirt. But you at the same time suddenly experience an overwhelming upsurge of joy. You are alive, you remember. You still walk above the ground. You breathe in the sun's unyielding light. You are thrilled that you aren't the poor corpse ready to be lowered. You revel in your good luck. Once again you feel as you did when you shook before the birth and the marriage. You feel an acutely curious melding of fear and hope, gloom and gladness. You are again immensely alive, a creature sharing in the cosmos's jangling polarities, its ubiquitous rises and dips.

These experiences—they are the most profound ones we can imagine—suggest that we are most deeply vital when we realize that joy and sorrow go together, that one cannot exist without the other. Becoming aware of this situation, we become further cognizant of the fact that all the universe likewise secretly brings together gasping antinomies. In apprehending this cosmic polarity, we feel as though we are at one with the world, that our own agitated unities are perfectly in synch with the chaotic concords of everything else. At such a moment we suffer what we can only call peace, grace, an innocent sensation that we were meant for this soul-rending earth, and it for us.

Stoked, as we know, by "nervous fear," William Blake was

perhaps more attuned to these mysteries than anyone else. Blake knew, for instance, that "without contraries there is no progression." He manifested this idea in his *Songs of Innocence and Experience* (1794), subtitled *Showing Two Contrary States of the Soul*. In his first section, "Songs of Innocence," Blake explores the strengths and weaknesses of innocence. On the one hand, innocence is a joyful spontaneity, untroubled bliss. On the other hand, innocence is delimiting ignorance, a kind of emotional immaturity. In his next section, Blake meditates on the virtues and vices of experience. Experience is of course a sorrowful sense of the world's tragic nature, a falling away from the happiness of innocence. But experience is also a wizened knowledge, an admirable gaze into the world's evils, complexities, and losses.

Blake's idea seems to be this: Innocence alone is inadequate; for all its happiness, it remains ignorant. Experience by itself is not good enough; despite its wisdom, it is bitter, cynical. Blake suggests that a third term is necessary, a paradoxical site, a kind of experienced innocence, a sort of spontaneous self-consciousness. Indeed, in an inscription on a manuscript page of his poem *The Four Zoas*, Blake claims that *true* innocence is one not with simple ignorance but rather with experienced wisdom: "Unorganizd Innocence, An Impossibility / Innocence dwells with Wisdom but never with Ignorance." These lines imply that true innocence is conscious of what it does, that it is curiously a mixture of freedom and discipline, childhood and adulthood. Fittingly, Blake hints at this sort of innocence in his *Songs*. As S. Foster

Damon, a great Blake critic, puts it, "A further state, a synthesis of [innocence and experience], is indicated in the 'Introduction' to *Songs of Innocence*, when the piper's tune makes the poet laugh, then weep, and the third time weep 'with joy.'" This third state is organized innocence, dynamic innocence. We experience this when we undergo that keen mixture of sadness and joy at births, weddings, and funerals.

It is our own nervous fear, our melancholia, that leads to our awareness of the world's innate duplicity, its "both/and." Only by being unwilling to rest on one side of the world or the other do we come to sense the hidden marriage between both sides. Sadly inhabiting this rich limbo, we put ourselves in a position to grasp the profound meaning of life's deepest events. These vexed events reveal to us what is already true of everything: all creatures are meldings of grandeur and gloom.

OF COURSE our American culture wants us to move to one side or the other, to label ourselves one thing or another—as introverts or extraverts, as brooders or boasters. Above all, the happy types of America want us to stay focused on the social side of things. Beaming with glad-handing happiness, they encourage us to get out in the world, to foster lasting friendships, to laugh it up with the boys, to take up a cause. But when these same citizens understand that we have a dark side, a side attuned to mulling over moons alone, they want us to stay safely in that quarter, to group with those few

Americans who have embraced melancholia. They want us to sidle up to those Emos or those Goths, those Grungers or those Satanists, small hordes making sadness their pastime.

This is one of the great bifurcations in American culture, between those who meet and greet and those who mull and scowl. One ultimately wonders if both sides are in fact flights from rich confusion into shallow clarity. Not wanting to endure the fecund, though difficult, limbo between two antinomies, most identify either with their intimate subjectivity or with the distance of objects. These masses would fixate on either an enduring self inside or the restless pulsations of the world outside. Doing so, these millions would break the universe in two—into gloominess or geniality, darkness or light—and favor one half. The majority of folk would divide and conquer. They would hold to one pole and annihilate the other. They would limp through life, half alive.

We realize that those committed to happiness at any cost and those bent on sadness no matter what are not very different from each other. Both are afraid of the wispy middle, that fertile and often febrile ambiguity between the poles of the cosmos. Both happy types and sad types can't endure the dusky limbo, so they leap to the lurid lucidity. Obviously, those happy types, bent only on bliss, always take flight from this complicated limbo. But those who have committed their lives to dejection are no different. These sad types—those black-clad poseurs who identify only with the darkness—choose sullenness as one picks a religion or a haircut. Like their brighter opponents, these self-consciously depressed

denizens cut half of life away. They too live only partial existences. These petulant performers gall us as much as do
the happy types. Where the happy types zig, they zag. When
the contented man says yes, they simply say no. These sad
types are controlled by their enemies, and they control their
foes. These dark types and happy types are secret bedfel-
lows, with one creating the other. Under the black trench lies
a T-shirt with a smile. Beneath the pastel lurks lament.

Our task is somehow to stay strong in the middle. We
don't want to live through fear, through fear of the perpetual
twilight from which both somber brooder and shiny optimist
run. We want to endure this murkiness. We want to be able
to stay up late and think through our confusions. We want
to discover a deep synthesis between the world's immense
antagonisms. We want to find the secret interdependence
between and among things, the untold concord covertly
holding together the cosmos. We want, for once, to know
that our pain will yield us a vision of rugged and vital unity
unavailable to those who live only for mere tranquillity, the
shallow peace.

We indeed want the peace that's deep, the profound tranquillity. We don't want the peace that comes with passive ac-
ceptance of the status quo. We don't desire the tranquillity of
resting comfortably on one side of the world or the other.
No. We want a capaciously complex repose. We hope to
know deep in our beings that the antinomies of the cosmos
exist through a dynamic accord, with one side continually in
complicit conflict with the other. The day pushes the night

to be blacker than it otherwise would be; the moon inspires the sun to shine more brightly than might be its wont. In the same way, durable melancholia reveals the secret of joy while ecstasy unveils the core of gloom. Sensing this interdependence, we feel ready to move this way or that, light on our feet, untroubled by a desire to grasp that side or this. We can play in the middle.

But there is an irony here: we cannot rest in this tranquillity. If we were to fixate on the temporary comfort of this vision, we would become superficial. We would ignore the pulsating polarities that generated the concord in the first place. We would become static, stable, contented—and as dead as the happy millions that we earlier avoided. No, sadly, we melancholy types cannot rest for long in our sudden joy. We must return to the work of vacillating between oppositions. We must understand that these oppositions relate to each other in many ways, multitudinous ways, and that we have discovered only one. To stay attuned to the flow of life, we must continue our explorations, our soundings of boundaries and thresholds. Doing this, we deepen our understandings of life's insoluble mysteries, its endless permutations between one thing and another.

This is the endless labor of the melancholy life. Just when we believe that we can come to rest in this worldview or that, we suddenly get that nervous feeling in our stomach or that strange crease in the brain. We realize that something's not quite right, that our recent insight is somehow inadequate to the world's overabundance, its rolling whales and its crows that are ghoulish, its intricate faces, labyrinthine, and its lost loves. Grimly we begin to question our stance, and indeed, we come to understand that it was really valuable for only a time. Up again, we say to ourselves, up again into the knockabout world, up again with very little conceptual armor, with only our quick wits to see us through. Insights, we realize, are like coats for the celeritous seasons; they are good for only a brief time. We are always searching for a new garment appropriate to the moment. This is hard labor, perpetual labor, but it is labor that will yield fruit, for only through relinquishing our secure theories can we open ourselves to the planet's vexed beauties, beauties that will spawn fresh insights into polarity's secrets, into life's conundrums.

So these visions of dynamic concord, if we are honest, are brief. However, they deepen our connection to what I can only call life. They, these visions of ephemeral peace, empower us to keep our melancholy acute in hopes of other profoundly healing moments. They help us trust the lubricious world. They inspire doubtful faith. They keep us honest and confused in a world of trivial liars.

MELANCHOLIA RETURNS us to what Emily Dickinson calls "possibility," a "fairer house than Prose / More Numerous of Windows / Superior for Doors." Pushing us into the fecund, though difficult, limbo between oppositions, it becomes a muse. It becomes a muse of understanding, of insight into the secret kinship between antinomies. It turns into a muse of vision, that perception of the state in which the polarities suddenly cohere into a turbulent concord. It functions as a muse of creativity, as a spur to create fresh ways of imagining these infinitely mysterious relationships between oppositions.

No one understood these muselike powers of melancholia more profoundly than Samuel Taylor Coleridge, the great nineteenth-century British poet. In the summer of 1805, aged thirty-two, almost in the middle of life's way, Coleridge found himself languishing in Malta, suspended among myriad possibilities. As the acting public secretary for the British governor of the island, Coleridge dangled between a temporary and a permanent position. But he also hovered between his former vocation as poet of England's northern lakes and his present one as bureaucrat in the sweltering Mediterranean. Softening the rigors of public work with doses of opium, Coleridge further vacillated between activity and reverie, the ledgers of daylight and the nocturnal notebook. In his hypnagogic memoranda, he pulsated between fervid accounts of the island's variety—its white rocks and crimson larkspurs, earthquakes and lucid stars— and abstract speculations on cosmic unity, thoughts on soul and life.

Enduring this endless limbo, Coleridge no doubt brooded over the terrible emotional upheavals that had thus far agitated his existence. He experienced the early death of a loving father. He suffered a long season essentially orphaned in a cold, cruel school for boys. He endured a bad marriage with a woman whom he did not love. He underwent unrequited affection from someone whom he felt to be his soul mate. He had a vexed friendship with William Wordsworth and a troubled relationship with his beloved son Hartley. These strains of the heart were matched by the body's difficulties: neuralgia, insomnia, constipation, night terrors, and opium addiction.

This ill fortune understandably fostered a melancholy disposition. This disposition frequently manifested itself in long bouts of lassitude, procrastination, and reverie— extreme seasons of heady paralysis. But Coleridge came to understand that these aberrant behaviors, these violations of the workaday status quo, these lengthy sessions of limbo, were the fields in which his imagination could play.

Coleridge made this melancholy edginess his vocation. He was incredibly successful. From about 1802, when he was thirty, until the end of his life—he died at the age of sixty-two—he repeatedly complained in his notebooks and letters of his impotent despair. He was horribly and constantly beset, he wrote, by a "melancholy dreadful feeling" that reduced him to a catatonic state. Numbed and sad, he could not capture the poetic glory of his youth, characterized by brilliant works like "Kubla Khan" (1797) and "The Rime of the Ancient Mariner" (1798). He could manage only, he confessed, "fruitless memoranda" on his "own Weakness."

This inability to do anything but dose on opium and jot mental meanderings was "Degradation," he believed, worse than even suicide. At least suicide, he thought, is doing *something*, even if the action is totally destructive. Coleridge was trapped in a gloomy limbo between what he wanted to do and what he could do. He could conclude only that his life was meaningless. "We all look up to the Sky for comfort, but nothing appears there—nothing comforts, nothing answers us—& so we die."

But out of this suffering arose brilliant passages on melancholia. In one striking sequence, Coleridge likened his pain to that of a fish struggling for life on some patch of shimmering mud, the ocean tantalizingly nearby. "The Fish gasps on the glittering mud, the mud of this once full stream, now only moist enough to be glittering mud / the tide will flow back, time enough to lift me up with straws & withered sticks and bear me down to the ocean. O me! That being what I have been I should be what I am!"

Another time he compared his blasted poetic gift with useless candle wax, once fiery but now cold and dead. "The Poet is dead in me—my imagination . . . lies, like Cold Snuff on the circular Rim of a Brass Candle-stick, without even a stink of Tallow to remind you that it was once cloathed and mitred with flame."

Yet another time his pain produced in him a tragically acute yearning for a paradise this earth cannot offer. "If a man could pass through Paradise in a Dream, & have a Flower presented to him as a pledge that his Soul had really been there, & found that Flower in his hand when he awoke—Aye! And what then?" More than a fantasy of return to Eden, this question goes beyond fancy to fact. Can one, through an act of soul, actually grasp a real paradise? Is it possible to create heaven on earth?

The fish floundering on the bejeweled mud, the poet as dead as forgotten and dusty candle wax, the man so desperate for solace that he begins to believe in the sweet flowers of his dreams: these sharply accurate images of melancholia came from the most potent muse, the muse of suffering. Had Coleridge not hated himself so, he never would have left behind these heartbreakingly beautiful and affectionate maps of the bewildering forests of sadness. He was hurt into these sublimities. He was axed into ecstasy.

Coleridge's understanding of his soul's deepest desires in the midst of horrible deprivations shows this: to grasp the core of any experience, one must desperately need to have this experience. The thirsty man knows water more keenly than does the sated one. Coleridge knew what the soul needs for solace more acutely than did the contented fellow. Realizing what the soul requires, he in his sadness offered a healing and a hope far more capacious and powerful than the paltry poultices and promises of the merely happy.

Was there a way, Coleridge wondered, to transcend his suffering? Unable to discover an escape with his outer eye, he turned to his inner vision. From this interior palace, he built beautiful ruins, strenuously innocent paeans to the powers of sad experience. He wrote original poems on the redemptions of melancholy, poems like "Dejection: An Ode" (1802) and "Limbo" (1811). In works like *Biographia Literaria* (1817), he crafted magically arcane philosophies devoted to dynamic unity. He discovered in his notebooks—late at night, frenzied with grief—the deep height of melancholia. He transmuted the dissolutions of despair into unforgettable gold.

COLERIDGE'S QUICK VISIONS of harmony, growing from the melancholy limbo and lasting only an instant, probably got him closer to the nerve and the gristle of life than anything else. For a brief period he likely felt perfectly at home in the cosmos, as though he were moving with the grain of organic growth and decay, as if he were oscillating between the crests and troughs of time.

This is another of the ironies of the melancholy existence. In feeling fractured and fragmented, isolated and bereft, one actually comes to experience wholeness and unity. To suffer melancholy is also to understand its polar opposite, joy. Lacking joy, one broods on it more deeply than when one possesses this state. Contemplating this condition, one eventually comes to understand it more profoundly than one would if one were actually experiencing joy. In vacillating between sorrow and joy, one grasps the secret harmony between these two antinomies. Doing so, one apprehends the rhythms of the whole cosmos, itself a dynamic interplay between opposites. To get this fact is to move close to the core of the world, to become acquainted with how the universe works and breathes and is. In such moments as this— those instants when we feel connected to the whole—we return, in a strange way, to innocence.

Innocence in this sense is not gullibility or naiveté. It is not the willingness to accept appearance as reality or delusion as truth. It is not childishness or stupidity. It is not lack of development or prepubescence. On the contrary, innocence in this context is what I can only call playfulness, a sense that the world is full of possibilities, that it is not fixed and stable and finished, that it thrives in the fertile middle ground that is not yet "this" or "that" but is in fact both "that" and "this" at once.

The best way to consider innocence in this way is to return to that great and tragic moment in the mythic consciousness of the Western world, the so-called fall and rise of man, the descent from blithe innocence to melancholy experience and then back again to innocence of another kind— innocence tempered by sadness, spontaneity limited by law. Let's recall the story. In this prefall condition, Adam and Eve were blissfully at peace with their environment. Adam so intimately knew the animals and plants that he could name them according to their true nature. He likewise was extremely close with Eve, a woman who was actually made of his own flesh and blood. Moreover, he was in concord with his own self; he knew at this time none of that shame that comes when a person sees himself through the judgmental eyes of others. Finally, he enjoyed concord with his deity. His God walked in the Garden of Eden to feel the sweet evening's coolness.

Then it was that these simple innocents, Adam and Eve, encountered for the first time a temptation to experience division. That's the essence of the emergence of the serpent. This creature with the appropriately forked tongue seduced Adam and Eve into believing that disunion is more exciting than mere unity. It opened their eyes to this possibility: to challenge the status quo—even though it might be handed down by God himself—is a more vital form of life than simply to accept the monotonous given. The serpent said to Eve, rebel against your god, for you might, in doing so, be able to access even greater worlds, to know things that you'll never even imagine here with these arbors and groves. Bold, Eve decided to partake of the serpent's knowledge, and then she convinced Adam to do the same. The fruit was good, succulent and perfectly ripe.

The instant Adam and Eve swallowed this fruit, their eyes became bright. They knew. They knew that the world was divided into evil and good, into light and darkness. Knowing this duplicity, they realized that other stupendous division, between self and self. They became self-conscious. They suddenly looked at themselves through the eyes of the other, and they felt shame. They covered their bodies with leaves.

Now divided against their very selves, Adam and Eve suffered other divisions. They understood that they could no longer simply converse with their god in the pleasant twilight. They would henceforth be divorced from him. They also realized that they would not experience perfect unity with each other. They placed barriers between themselves and grew suspicious one of the other. They moreover grasped this fact: they were separate from their environment and would have to battle the elements all their days.

Thus began the melancholy existence of Eve and Adam, an existence that they themselves actually chose. They picked division over unity because they hungered for more vitality than simple innocence offered. They wanted a world in which oppositions jostle and jump, in which one is never quite sure what will happen next. But this rich profusion came at a cost. From the moment that they consumed the fruit of knowing, they were doomed to suffer the ills of self-consciousness, that mental state that breeds endless agitation, persistent questioning, and ongoing doubt.

This is the double edge of the fall. On the one hand, it opened Adam and Eve to a more animated life, one replete with creative swerves and clangors. On the other hand, it constrained the first man and woman to a melancholy existence, a personal history filled with gnawing apprehensions and inquiries that hurt. If we are honest with ourselves, this is perhaps precisely the tension we feel right now—between joy in vivid agitation, life's unpredictable curves and swoops, and sadness over chronic insecurity, the ceaseless doubts of any existence authentically open to what new thing is coming next.

This, then, is the happy fall, the *felix culpa*. Only through falling from perfect and eternal concord can one enter into the turbid flow of time. Only by letting go of deathless existence can one actually experience endless life. Think of it. After Adam and Eve fell, they for the first time knew in their bones what goodness was. They could know this only by undergoing evil. Likewise, only after the fall could they know, deep down, what joy was. They could understand this only by suffering sorrow.

Indeed, Adam and Eve could understand innocence only by losing innocence. Experience is the path to innocence. Bereft of that perfect feeling of unity with everything—we all felt it in childhood—we pine for a vision approximating this concord. Pining, we understand this harmony more deeply than when we possessed it. We know, however, that we can't simply return to the old innocence; that was boring, vapid, predictable, the life of a babe. We long now to experience another sort of innocence, that innocence that grows from experience, that partially and briefly redeems from experience, that for an instant takes us away from the struggle and the strife, from the perpetual and sometimes painful play between opposites.

This sort of innocence can come only when we are divided within ourselves, when we feel, acutely, the melancholy divisions that tortured and stimulated Adam and Eve. Suspended in a limbo between opposing powers, we long for a sudden vision of concord between these two potencies. We don't want a flat unity, one that's simply a rehash of that childish harmony we once enjoyed. No. We want a *dynamic* unity, one that allows the antinomies to remain active, fresh, alive. This sort of unity would be innocence tempered by experience, grace spiced by sin.

When does this sudden vision come? When we least expect it. But we all know what it feels like. Tense, consumed by blues, keen on relief, we choose to do something we love. We play the oboe or tend our peonies or compose a poem or undertake a walk in the woods. Initially, we can't take our minds off our unease. We remain self-conscious, painfully cognizant that we are aware of what we are doing, as though we were two creatures, one visible and acting, the other invisible and watching. While one side actually engages in ac-

tivity, the other side looks to the past with nostalgia or regret
or to the future with fear or anticipation. In this way we are
not fully present in the present. We are there and not there,
blooded and ghostly at once. This is the expansion and the
friction of self-consciousness. This is the transcendence and
the attenuation of the fall.

But after a while, for no apparent reason, we get into a
good rhythm of playing or gardening or writing or hiking,
and we forget ourselves. We no longer suffer the feeling of
division, of witnessing ourselves as though from above. It is
as if the phantom eye had sunk back down into the body.
Now we no longer look behind with longing or dissatisfaction or ahead with anxiety or expectation. We have inhab-
ited the present with our presence. Indeed, we feel that we,
in that moment, are one with the instant. We are not anymore troubled by past or future, by time itself. We are, in a
very real way, in eternity, a state that simply exists when a
person is not torn by time. This is dynamic innocence, not
the naive and childish innocence of yore but the mature and
knowing innocence of the adult, the innocence growing
from and relieving experience, the innocence that brings together and heals the rifts of the hellishly gorgeous world.

What can this hard-earned innocence be but grace, a quick
respite from the trammels of time? This is, to be sure, what
Adam and Eve learned from their fall. God can exert his grace
only in the face of sin. Mercy can flow only where it is needed.
One can know the light only from the position of darkness.

Through their exuberant melancholia, Adam and Eve
indeed apprehended the difficult joys of earning redemption.

Through their absence from literal Eden, they found the invisible Eden dwelling in their own hearts. Through their nakedness and solitude, they came to weave beautiful and attractive tapestries. Without their hunger for the sorrowful knowledge, none of this would have occurred. They would have remained as children, obedient and cowering.

WHETHER WE BELIEVE in the Genesis myth or not, all of us, no matter what our dispositions are, probably feel that we have fallen into a difficult, though exhilarating, world. How can we escape melancholia in an existence in which we are doomed to suffer physical and psychical pain, perturbing hours and miles that are arduous? If we are honest, we cannot. But isn't it precisely this melancholia that gives life its edge, its friction, its exquisite frisson? Indeed, if not for the troublous gloom of our lives beyond the gates of Eden, we would never pine for a richer version of innocence than we had in childhood. We would never achieve experiences of this fertile innocence. We would never endeavor to create new ways of attaining this dynamically blissful, though tragically transient, vision.

More than anything, our consciousness of our fallen state makes us innovative. When we feel content with the status quo, we have no need to be creative. We can simply imitate the given and be tranquil. However, when we honestly suffer the constraints of our limited and bifurcated condition, bracing though it is, we yearn to fashion fresh freedoms and original unities. We specifically hope to discover novel ways of envisioning relationships between the oppositions enlivening us even as they tear us asunder. We want to empower ourselves with new descriptions, to see the world anew.

It is 1952. A polio epidemic has just spread through the cold towns of Canada. A young girl named Roberta Joan Anderson is unexpectedly laid low by the disease. She is only nine years old. She finds herself in a hospital. The season is winter, just around Christmastime. Her parents and others, worried sick, come to visit her regularly. She is told that she might not ever be able to walk again and that she definitely will not be able to go home for Christmas. Roberta is pained to the point of tears, terrified and despondent. But then, just when her despair is deepest, she decides to bring Christmas to her hospital room. Though she is confined to her bed, she begins to belt out carols, sending her vibrant Christmas ecstasy abroad. Her horror of being divorced from the evergreens and the dances makes her sing all the louder. She is pained into song.

Some years later, when she was in her early twenties, after she had, by pure luck, regained her ability to walk and had developed into an accomplished guitar player and singer, Roberta—soon to go by her stage name, Joni Mitchell, and also soon to be world famous—became pregnant. She decided to have the child. In February 1965 she gave birth to Kelly Dale Anderson, a girl. Young and confused and ambitious, Roberta, now Joni, put her child up for adoption. This experience of choosing to be separated from her infant shattered her. Much of the melancholy of Mitchell's early songwriting was informed by a pervasive sense of loss. As she later confessed to the media, "Bad fortune changed the course of my destiny. I became a musician." Yet again time's terrible lacerations wounded her into soulful carolings.

An early product of Mitchell's acute sorrow appeared in 1971, in one of her first great albums, titled, aptly, *Blue*. By this time she had spent several years on the folk scene. She had in fact already cut three fairly successful folk albums, *Song to a Seagull* (1968), *Clouds* (1969), and *Ladies of the Canyon* (1970). But none of these albums possesses the disconsolate lilts of *Blue*, a series of tracks devoted to the longing and failure and loneliness and dissatisfaction of a deeply lived life. Mitchell herself noted the pensive vulnerability of the piece: "At that period of my life, I had no personal defenses. I felt like a cellophane wrapper on a pack of cigarettes. I felt like I had absolutely no secrets from the world and I couldn't pretend in my life to be strong." But it was this very weakness, this humble acknowledgment of the power of her pain, that drove Mitchell into her strong intonings, her full-hearted pulsations.

The album is full of songs devoted to world-weary and strung-out lovers stunned by their losses. In the album's final cut, "The Last Time I Saw Richard," the singer, after detailing the wasted life of an old friend, feels the futility of her own life of torn fantasies. She concludes the piece by receding into solitude in a bleak café, confessing that she doesn't want to talk to anyone. Brooding alone, she silently observes that this café is a place through which dreamers will pass; moving through, they will hide in shame. She hopes that her own time in this café will serve as a gloomy womb from which she might emerge, reborn and ready to fly. In an earlier track, titled "Blue," the singer sends a desperate song of love to a distant lover named Blue. She notes that this man has suffered the jagged tides of life and tried to escape them through a litany of chemicals and illicit activities. He now dwells in a kind of hell, into which the singer, like Orpheus, is willing to descend in hopes of saving him. Her love, her wistful love, she believes, might bring him to the light. To commemorate this forlorn love, she leaves Blue this sorrowful song. In the most melancholy cut on the album, "River," Mitchell returns to the Christmas season that she loved so much as a child. Now, though, she finds the season cruel, for all it does is remind her of her alienation and privation. She wishes only to avoid the forced good cheer. As she watches people cut down trees and put up reindeer and sing songs of cheer, she dreams of having a frozen-over river on which she can skate away.

Each of these songs—and there are others—reflects Mitchell's overall sense of her life. In a somewhat recent interview, she admits that she has frequently been laid low by depression. However, she has not shied away from the darkness. She calls her persistent melancholia the "sand that makes the pearl" and acknowledges the fact that some of her "best work" has emerged from her troubled emotions. She goes on to say that she always knew that she should never fully exorcise her darkness. She has realized over the years this: "chase away the demons, and they will take the angels with them."

Mitchell's life, leading to this insight about the relationship between demons and angels, reveals yet another point about the melancholy life. Melancholy living shows us that our demons—the dark parts of our hearts, our agitations and our loathings, our cynicisms and our acerbities—are integral parts of ourselves, absolutely essential. Indeed, it is our acidity that actually makes us unique individuals. As Tolstoy famously says, all happy families are exactly the same. The same is true of people: in conforming to standards of goodness, they end up behaving in more or less the same fashion. It is only our struggle with what Alan Watts calls our "irreducible element of rascality" that distinguishes us from others. Show me your "good side," your visage in only a happy light, and I see only a general principle at work. Show me your bad side, and I shall know you, for it is precisely this side that unveils your personal and private strife.

As Mitchell suggests, if we were to get rid of our bad lights, our demons, then our other parts, our so-called good parts, would leave us as well. At that point we would become mere masks painted over with grins. We must then tenaciously grasp our darknesses, our faults. To hold to these nether regions of our beings is to understand an individual vitality, an unrepeatable force. Understanding this energy, we come to apprehend in a new context the hidden connection between somberness and shining. We realize once more that melancholy is the chaos birthing fresh creations. This discord is a roiling ocean constantly conjuring gorgeous whirlpools and eddies that are silver. The hectic gives birth to elegance.

COLERIDGE AND MITCHELL, children of Ficino, are but a few of the many sad souls who put their bouts with paralysis and privation and perturbation to good use. Each endures the limbo. Each grasps the secret marriage of sorrow and joy. Each creates out of this insight original products. These melancholy creatures constitute a fascinating team of mentors. To contemplate these guides in a dark time is to garner the strength to endure. We all can identify with these great beings, an honor roll of brilliant men and women.

We think of writers like Ernest Hemingway and Rita Dove, musicians like Beethoven and Mahler, painters such as Goya and van Gogh. But not only artists; we also recall politicians such as Lincoln and Churchill, entrepreneurs like J. C. Penney and Ted Turner, actors like Carrie Fisher and Jim Carrey. We moreover think of scientists like Isaac Newton and Sigmund Freud and military leaders like Napoléon and Sherman.

I could add others to this august list of melancholy innovators. I could mention Martin Luther and Michelangelo, Hart Crane and F. Scott Fitzgerald, Hans Christian Andersen and Florence Nightingale, James M. Barrie and Mary Shelley, Handel and Holst, Rossini and Schumann, Paul Gauguin and Edvard Munch. I could further note Noël Coward, Victor Hugo, Pyotr Ilich Tchaikovsky, Charles Ives, Leo Tolstoy, Virginia Woolf, Dylan Thomas, and Søren Kierkegaard.

These lists don't even come close to doing justice to the great honor roll of creative melancholics. What about Alfred

Lord Tennyson, Franz Kafka, and Jackson Pollock? What about Abbie Hoffman, Tennessee Williams, and William Faulkner? What about John Lennon? What about Ad Reinhardt? What about Cary Grant? What about Marcel Proust?

If you are right now suffering constant melancholia, you are included in this fascinating litany of profound men and women. You are sick of the status quo. You want something more out of life than the flaccid conventions offer. You are edgy, slightly afraid. But you feel in this moment more alive than ever before. You sense that you are on the verge of imagining alternative worlds, untapped powers. In your moment of fecundity, you look toward these figures as guides to the unmapped land. They speak in your quivering ear moving mantras. The mainstream reduces mystery to material. Easy contentment is craven. To grasp convention is to forsake force. Despondency is durable. *Duende* is delight.

But isn't there finally something sinister about many of these innovators? Many committed suicide. We know all the stories. In 1890, Vincent van Gogh brought his most frenzied period of creativity to an abrupt and violent close. After manically completing upward of two hundred paintings between 1888 and 1890, including his great *Starry Night* and *Crows in the Wheatfields*, van Gogh, deeply depressed, walked out into the gorgeous yellow sun of the southern French landscape and shot himself in the gut with a pistol. He died from the wound two days later. He was thirty-seven.

On April 27, 1932, Hart Crane was once again drunk. He was also smarting, physically hurting from a beating he had received from a male crew member toward whom he had made a sexual advance and psychically aching over his life-long depression, his thwarted homosexuality, the poor reviews of his 1930 poetic masterwork *The Bridge*. He was on a steamer bound from Mexico, where he had just finished up a Guggenheim fellowship, to New York City, the place where he lived. He would never make it, however, to his beloved city. Just before noon on this late April day, he stepped over the ship's railing, fell into the Gulf of Mexico, and drowned at the age of thirty-three.

In late February 1970 the painter Mark Rothko, aged sixty-seven, was undergoing several maladies, material and spiritual. His health was bad. His wife of many years had recently left him. He felt that his recent art was inferior to his earlier work. No longer was he able to achieve those transcendently luminous squares of his middle years, those angular portals to something beyond, hovering, up there, in space. About all he could muster as he neared the winter of 1970 was this gnomic saying, the "dark is always at the top." On February 25, Rothko's assistant found the man lying on the floor of his kitchen, dead. He had opened the veins of his wrists. The razor lay at his side.

Addictions have also hounded many of these creators. Several, like Coleridge, could not, during their lifetimes, shake nagging obsessions with alcohol or drugs. Faulkner interspersed into his frenzied periods of writing long bouts of drinking. Pollock as he approached his fateful car crash was rarely sober. Cary Grant needed serious psychotherapy, helped by LSD, to wean himself from the bottle. Freud incessantly used cocaine. Abbie Hoffman, though a genius for political activism, constantly fought heroin addiction. Likewise, Lennon, amid penning his brilliantly bitter lyrics, frequently battled a drug and alcohol habit.

Are suicidal urges and dangerous addictions the price to be paid for melancholy genius? Not in all cases, of course, but certainly the high number of melancholy innovators who struggled with serious despair and sordid habits is revealing. It's perhaps easy to admire these creators from afar; their selfishness and dejection produced beauties that nourish us no end. But what of those close to these strung-out inventors? What of their spouses and their children, their friends and their relatives? What would they think of my words praising these avant-garde makers as noble hearts? They would likely say that I'm romanticizing melancholia, making it more palatable than it really is. They would probably further say that I'm being unfair to those who suffered all those long and tearful nights mourning or medicating those broken-down souls.

These would be legitimate criticisms. I admit that I'm probably being overly generous to these destructive types because of what they've left behind. I wonder if the melancholy innovator must be selfish so that the rest of us, if we attend well to his or her work, can learn to be more generous, open, flexible—moral. If this is the case, then it is perhaps one of the great and enduring tragedies of our planet. People must suffer for beauty. This treasure comes at a serious price. As Emily Dickinson says, great and lasting art is the "gift of screws." This means that durable beauty must be broken and wrung, squeezed until its very life comes oozing out.

This is perhaps a mystery with which we must simply live and, in living with it, continue to admire those melancholy souls who have devoted their lives to the creation of beauty, no matter what the cost. This is finally what encourages us to indulge these calamitous creators, to treat them almost as we would treat deities, as though they were somehow above our normal codes of behavior. And we tend to do this not just because these dangerous souls grant us heavenly gifts. We embrace these creatures also because they aggrandize our own struggles with the blues, showing us that our sadness is not aberrant or unseemly or weakness but instead a call to interior depths, to cauldrons out of which will bubble new solutions, crimson and sweet and unforgettable.

These beautiful spumes feel something like grace, light emerging from the dark nadir. And this is the core of the matter. We in the end are forgiving of these melancholy spirits, even though they destroy themselves and us, because we know that out of their suffering emerge things rich and strange.

Melancholia is the profane ground out of which springs the sacred. Our hope that this claim is valid is what keeps most of us tenderly disposed toward the sadness of others, no matter how indulgent, and the gloom of our own hearts, regardless of the pain. We have a faith that the dejection will lead to affirmation. If we go on living without this embrace of the darkness, then we are left with the most horrific of situations: suffering is meaningless. If this were true, we likely could not long persist. We need to believe that our shadows generate the light. We must hold to this position. It is consent to the given, a graceful grasp of gravity, a yea to the thunderous no.

Creating doesn't make us unhappy; unhappiness makes us creative. To create is to live, and in living, we want only to create more, to set our foundations deeper and reach higher toward the sky. If sadness is what makes us creative, then sadness is nothing else but life. Frowning is flourishing. The grouch is the "ought," the impetus to vigor. Plumb down into your interiors. There find the sullen ruler of the underworld. On his face is an ambiguous grimace. It is possibly a clenched product of the somber darkness. But it is more likely a squinting before the amber glow growing before his eyes.

TERRIBLE BEAUTY

Melancholy is at the bottom of everything, just as at the
end of all rivers is the sea. Can it be otherwise in a
world where nothing lasts, where all that we have loved
or shall love must die? Is death, then, the secret of
life? The gloom of an eternal mourning enwraps,
more or less closely, every serious and thoughtful
soul, as night enwraps the universe.
—HENRI FRÉDÉRIC AMIEL

ON NOVEMBER 30, 1820, as the autumn orange de-
cayed into earth's winter muck, John Keats, suffering from the tuberculosis that killed his mother and his
brother Tom, sat down to draft a letter to his good friend
Charles Brown. This was to be his last known correspon-
dence. Between horrific bouts of coughing—coughing that
stained his tongue with blood—Keats recovered himself
enough to write these striking lines: "I have an habitual feeling of my real life having past, and that I am leading a

posthumous existence." At the age of twenty-five, when he should have been relishing multitudinous opportunities for love and for growth, for summer's larks and pretty girls, Keats already felt like a corpse. It seemed to him as though he were already in the grave and therefore looking back on his days as one would witness a character in a finished story. There he was, composing, viewing the world with a dead man's eyes.

While he was creating this epistle, Keats no doubt brooded over his brief life. When he was but nine years old, his father, while riding home from a visit, fell from his horse and died the very next day. After only a few years had passed, his mother was, as I've mentioned, diagnosed with tuberculosis. Though Keats nursed her assiduously, sitting up with her all hours of the night, cooking for her, reading to her, she succumbed in 1810, during Keats's fifteenth year. Orphaned, Keats was assigned to a guardian and soon after taken from a beloved boarding school and required to apprentice as an apothecary. Keats found the work to be tedious, for during these years, his late teen years, he was awakening to the grandeurs of poetry, especially the verse of Spenser and Shakespeare. To complete his training, Keats had to learn surgery during the years 1815 and 1816. Day after day he toiled in a hospital, malodorous and bloody, where he witnessed nothing but suffering. As he increasingly turned from surgery and toward poetry, he completed his first substantial poem, *Endymion*, which he published in 1818. Two of the leading literary magazines of the time attacked the poem for not making sense. Around this time Keats's brother Tom

died after a long and painful period of illness. While attending Tom, Keats met the love of his life, Fanny Brawne. He
became engaged to her in 1819. However, he soon realized
that he would never be able to marry her because he himself
was doomed to fall prey to the same disease that killed his
family members. He knew he would die without ever con-
summating his ardent love.

One would think that Keats's tragic life would have fostered in him an extreme bitterness, a petulance born of persistent unfairness. But Keats, much to his credit and almost
miraculously, remained generous in the face of his difficulties. Indeed, he weathered life's blows as though he were in a
sense already dead, posthumous, someone who could somehow transcend suffering and despair even as he underwent
the horrific calamities.

This is the essence of his announcement that he felt
"posthumous." The statement suggests that Keats near the
end of his life was not rancorous toward his misfortunes.
Rather, as he approached his demise, he was strangely detached from life's perpetual ills. He could basically say that
he was in the race and out of the race at the same time, both
engrossed by the sense of his impending death and disjoined
from this same sensibility. He could endure the bludgeons of
time while at the same time not caring about the contusions.

To be sure, it says something about Keats that he didn't
flee to the usual escapes that offered themselves in the early
nineteenth century: Christianity or opium, drink or dreaming. Though he unsurprisingly underwent pangs of serious
melancholia (who wouldn't, faced with his disasters?), he

nonetheless remained sturdy in the face of his abiding woe. He never fell into self-pity or self-indulgent sorrow. In fact, he consistently transformed his gloom, grown primarily from his experiences with death, into a vital source of beauty. Things are gorgeous, he often claimed, *because* they die. The porcelain rose is not as pretty as the one that decays. Melancholia over time's passing is the proper stance for beholding beauty. Mourning makes the dead dawn brightly shine.

Why would Keats do such a seemingly perverse thing? Why would he actually embrace decay and the consequent heartaches? He did so because he understood that suffering and death are not aberrations to be cursed but necessary parts of a capacious existence, a personal history attuned to the plentiful polarity of the cosmos. To deny calamity and the corpse would be to live only a partial life, one devoid of creativity and beauty. Keats welcomed his death so that he could live.

Taking this double stance—suffering death while transcending death—Keats was in his pain and above his pain. He could refuse it and hold it at once. He could at the same time loathe it and love it. He could fear it and see the beauty in it. Keats developed this interplay between detachment and attachment in one of his most famous letters, the one on the "vale of Soul-making." In this 1819 epistle, penned at the bleak nadir of his tragic life, Keats asks the following question: "Do you not see how necessary a World of Pains and troubles is to school an Intelligence and make it a Soul?" He's here implying that an abstract mind can develop into a full-hearted person only through enduring long periods of sadness and pain. Only a person who could accept the world as it is, a place of sorrow as much as joy, would say such a thing. Keats is acutely aware of the difficulty of becoming a human being in this world, but he also realizes, as though he were beyond the agony, that the pain is absolutely necessary.

In another famous letter, this one from 1818, Keats compares a human's life with a "large Mansion of Many Apartments." He states that the only way to engage the great mysteries of life is to suffer "Misery and Heartbreak, Pain, Sickness and oppression." Undergoing these troubles, one moves from the "Chamber of Maiden Thought," the room of innocence, into darker passages, the regions of profound experience. In this latter place, one finds the inspiration for poetry, poetry that explores the mysterious burdens of life. In this case, too, Keats shows himself to be intensely aware of the painful world but also keenly willing to embrace this same pain. It's as if once more he were somehow in the world but not of it, able to suffer the troublous gloom but also able to see beyond it. He's able to see beyond it, we soon learn, because this pain is the muse of beauty.

KEATS MAKES THIS POINT in a poem, "Ode on Melancholy," from 1819. This poem begins with Keats calling us to hold hard to our melancholy moods. He urges us not to alleviate our blues with befuddling chemicals. He also calls on us not to escape our suffering through suicide. Finally, he makes a plea for us not to become so melancholy that all that we can think of are yewberries, death-moths, and morbid owls. If we do any of these things, then we'll dull the edge of melancholia. We'll "drown the wakeful anguish of the soul."

Keats next explores the result of keeping our melancholy keen. Remaining conscious of our dark moods, we might fall into a "melancholy fit," a deep experience of life's transience but also of its beauty. Fittingly, this melancholy fit is a mixed affair. It falls from heaven like a "weeping cloud, / That fosters the droop-headed flowers all." That is, this fit is a blend of gloom—clouds and wilting flowers—and of vitality: rain and nourishment. Indeed, this cloud "hides the green hill in an April shroud." This strongly suggests that the melancholy fit is a meeting of fertility and decay.

What can we call this fit but a meaningful experience of generative melancholy, of that strange feeling that sadness connects us to life's vibrant pulses? Alienated from home and happiness, we sense what is most essential: not comfort or contentment but authentic participation in life's grim interplay between stinking corpses and singing lemurs. This experience is a "fit." It shivers our souls.

In this tense mood we are in a position to understand the relationship between beauty and death. Keats urges us while in this condition to "glut" our sorrow on a "morning rose" or "on the rainbow of the salt sand-wave" or "on the wealth of globed peonies." He then says that if our "mistress" shows "rich" anger, we should take her hand and let her "rave" and "feed deep, deep upon her peerless eyes."

What do these recommendations have in common? Each features the melancholy soul experiencing something beautiful but also something transient, a quick rose or an ephemeral rainbow or peonies that perish or a mistress's flashing eyes. The suggestion appears to be this: there is a connection among melancholy, beauty, and death.

Keats makes this connection clear in the next sequence. He tells us that this mistress and, by implication, those roses and rainbows and peonies all dwell with beauty, beauty "that must die." These elements also live with joy, "whose hand is ever at his lips / Bidding adieu; and aching Pleasure nigh, / Turning to poison while the bee-mouth sips." Indeed, in the "temple of Delight, / Veiled Melancholy has her sovran shrine." No one can witness this shrine but the person "whose strenuous tongue" has "burst Joy's grape against his palate fine." This person will taste the "sadness" of melancholy's "might." He will be among her "cloudy trophies hung."

These associations make for several conclusions. The "wakeful anguish" of sharp melancholia can lead to a shuddering experience, a "fit." This vital moment grows from an insight into the nature of things: life grows from death; death gives rise to life. This insight animates melancholy, makes it vibrant. But it also intensifies the pain, for it emphasizes this: everything, no matter how beautiful, must die. Rather than flee from this difficult position, the melancholic appreciates things all the more *because* they die. Appreciating these things, the melancholic enjoys their beauty. In enjoying the beauty of the world, the melancholic himself wants to create beauty, to become a trophy that commemorates his resplendent experience of earth's transient gorgeousness.

MELANCHOLIA EMPOWERS US to experience beauty. When I say beauty, I don't mean the Hallmark beauty, prettiness, really: those perfect sunsets on the coastal horizon or those tranquil panoramas from the rounded top of a mountain or those perfectly airbrushed faces, wrinkle free and vacant. The beauty I have in mind is something much wilder: the violent ocean roiling under the tepidly peaceful beams or the dark and jagged peaks that bloody the hands or those unforgettable faces, striking because of a disproportionate nose or mouth that somehow brings the whole visage into a uniquely dynamic harmony.

Think of it. All pretty things are almost exactly alike, while all beautiful events are distinct. Prettiness, the manifestation of American happiness, is devoted to predictability and smoothness. The pretty view has no dangerous edges; the pretty face features no unexpected distortions. Don't all postcards give off a similar idea, that nature is a tranquil scene merely to be enjoyed by humans? Don't all supermodels look almost exactly alike, as if they were produced on some perfumed assembly line? We can go further: pretty things suggest a kind of emptiness. The mountain range reduced to a harmlessly fungible square of paper seems devoid of portentous power and foreboding threat. The human face is painted as a deserted gaze corresponding to the untenanted skull within; the bland expression is an extension of bland thoughts. Prettiness, then, with its halfhearted focus on sleekness and blankness, is finally a denial of the organic world—that serrated mess, that community that's craggy. And being a denial of organicity, this same prettiness is really an avoidance of death, a feeble hope that one can somehow escape the lacerations of time.

Beauty, on the other hand, is organic. The beautiful object is unpredictably mottled, scabrous, and fractured. The beautiful vista is indeed teeming with ominous waves and cloud-rending peaks. Likewise, the beautiful face from certain angles looks even homely, what with its lines and its asymmetries, but then, suddenly, in the right light, it all comes together into a ravishing vision. These interesting events, motley and slightly aberrant, seem to be expressions of equally interesting powers. The rough sea appears to manifest some magnificently afflicted organic principle. The intricate face in the same way probably corresponds to a nimble and flexible mind within. This ocean, this face: both are ultimately beautiful because they reveal the death within them. The turbulent sea threatens destruction as much as creation; the pied visage shows decay as well as growth.

Indeed, you can experience beauty only when you have a melancholy foreboding that all things in this world die. The transience of an object makes it beautiful, and its transience is manifested in its fault lines, its expressions of decrepitude. To go in fear of death is to forgo beauty for prettiness, that flaccid rebellion against corrosion. To walk with death in your head is to open the heart to peerless flashes of fire.

So, it should by now be obvious you can't discover beauty when you join the vacationing masses in search of poster aesthetics. Indeed, these folks—almost all of them happy types—can't really perceive beauty at all. All that they see is their expectation of the picture-perfect shot, pretty and presentable. They go to the mountains or the coast with numerous images downloaded into their heads. When they reach their destinations, they're not out to experience the strange terrain, the uncanny upsurges of gorgeous weirdness. They're rather in search only of occurrences that match their paper-thin minds. In this way, these scenery freaks don't get the world at all. All they notice is what they expect to witness, static shots of a Photoshopped globe.

The novelist Walker Percy, probably with Blake's take on the particular somewhere in his mind, discusses precisely this problem. In his essay "The Loss of the Creature" (1954), Percy argues that most go through life witnessing not the actual world but their preconceptions of it. Millions each year go to the Grand Canyon hoping for a sublime vision of nature's grandeur. However, these same millions have for years studied the canyon from afar, in postcards, posters, and photographs. These simulations of reality eventually encode in the many brains ideal images of the scene. When these masses finally muster the energy to go to the Grand Canyon, they never truly get to see the vast chasm. Instead, all they really perceive is their prefabricated picture of the place, their safely sentimental rendering. Indeed, many of these tourists come away from the actual canyon disappointed. They feel that the real canyon didn't quite measure up to their internal portrait. They feel that they didn't get the experience they really wanted. They feel cheated, slightly disdainful.

This same problem occurs in many contexts. Most students go to their biology classes believing that they will learn something about basic anatomy. Their professor gives them frogs to dissect. As the students go to work with their scalpels, they don't actually see frogs at all. All they perceive are the abstract anatomical relationships that the frogs exemplify. The particular frog is not a being in and of itself, a spotted olive sheen from which protrude indifferent eyes; it is simply a "specimen" of anatomy. The same occurs in English classes. Students arrive thinking that they might come to understand the nature of the sonnet. The professor distributes one day Keats's first great poem, a sonnet, "On First Looking into Chapman's Homer." Along with the professor, the students quickly try to learn just how this poem serves as a sonnet, is a "specimen" of a sonnet. Doing so, these students miss the unrepeatable concreteness of Keats's work, its striking idiosyncrasies, its images that are unforgettable, its eventful rhymes.

Percy offers a useful recommendation: biology teachers should one day surprise their students with sonnets, and English instructors should of a day startle their classes with dead frogs. Such unorthodox behavior would shock students out of their complacency, their dependence on safe abstractions, and force them to stare at things unadorned—beautiful and strange. Denuded of their habitual internal images, these students would have nothing to protect them from the world's gorgeous weirdness. Once overwhelmed with this torqued upsurge, these same students would likely work for the remainder of their days to surprise themselves, to strain through their familiar grids. They would go to the Louvre in hopes of breaking through their years of T-shirts and postcards and actually experience the enigmatic wantonness of the *Mona Lisa*. They would travel to Mont Blanc dreaming of the vertigo of altitudinous snow.

But these students, perhaps poor and pining with love, would prove the rare exception. Sadly, the loss of the real affects millions of folks every year. It's as if the masses had decided to eat menus instead of real food or consume money instead of what it can buy. They probably relinquish the world in hopes of remaining contented, safe, untroubled by the eerie dawn, the preternatural twilight. They wish for their lives to be one long vacation; they want to be perennial tourists. Remaining safely behind the objects of the gift shop, they stay separated from that shocking and tottering world that would depress them as much as buoy them, that would remind them of their own beautiful ugliness and their own living deaths.

All of us, obviously, go through the world with expectations. We face each day hoping that certain experiences will occur. However, we melancholy types, stoked on Keats and committed to learning, are aware that our preconceptions can block our access to the outlandishly novel world. Like those poor students at the Louvre or on Mont Blanc, we try as hard as we can to let go of our prefabricated grids and behold the world devoid of ourselves. When we do, we are amazed at what we find, a world whose deathly deformities cohere into durable pulchritude. Finding this, we begin to feel our own deaths pulsing in our veins. We realize that it is precisely these deaths that give us our unique and comely appearance. We try to embrace, then, the sad fact that the world most wants to forget: we all die, and in our dying is, paradoxically, our living.

AMERICA IS OBSESSED with forgetting this sad fact. Think of the country's collective, 85 percent of the people wearing a pretty grin to cover the beautiful grind of life. After a while, most come to think of this painted smile as the real thing. Doing so, the majority are rather easily able to reduce earth's tragedies into safe clichés, lazy chitchat.

An example of this flattening of the vital real to the boring idle is this: happy types tend to reduce the world's terrible tragedies—its wars, its hungers—to mindless talk on a television screen. While the earth struggles under its burdens, happy types tune in to pundits thundering over which side is right, the conservatives or the liberals, the war supporters or the peace lovers. The real issues are lost in all the talk. This is comforting, though, to happy types, who, after watching the shouting politicos, always have something to say about the worst crises. Reflecting the thoughts of the collective, those bent on happiness can pretend to understand and control barely bearable complexities. These types can always take a side and have something seemingly important to say.

Happy types tend to boil down their own problems in the same way. When they experience those terrible longings for what has been lost, when they feel those difficult hatreds toward what can never come back, then they fall into some clichéd affirmation about how they're good people and deserve to be happy. Or they recite some smarmy poem like Mary Stevenson's "Footprints in the Sand." Or they pray to some kind presence sitting idly in the sky. Or they take down their favorite book on happiness, or a devotional manual, or that bestseller on the wisdom of children. They pull themselves once more into that contented feeling. They go out into the world again beaming with all their might.

If only these types could learn to sit long with their inevitable anxieties. Regardless of how much they repress or ignore or forget, they must feel in their bones what all of us feel, fear of their own demise. This ubiquitous anxiety besets every conscious individual. There's no escaping it. When we think even for a minute about the nature of the universe, we remember that everything is rushing toward annihilation, and we become anxious about our own deaths. Surprised by this sudden anxiety, we can do one of two things. We can quickly flee from this feeling into the land of indolent babble, that flatland where everything ultimately is good. Or we can sit with our anxiety and let it pervade our hearts and thus honestly encounter our own finitude.

Anxiety indeed pushes us to consider the relative shortness of our lives. What are we always anxious about, either directly or indirectly, but our own end? Whether we are careworn over losing our jobs or being bereft of control or becoming alienated from a loved one, we always ultimately fear pain, and what is pain but a precursor to the last pain, death? When we are forced to face the fact that our existences are but mere blips on the scale of cosmic time, we realize how absolutely precious every instant is. We understand that we have only a very short time remaining to us and that we'd better make the best of it. In this way, just when we experience our extreme limitation, we also become aware of our grand possibilities. We want, more than anything, to live hard and full, to do what we've never done but only dreamed.

Feeling, in our nerves, this finitude, we enjoy, perhaps for the first time, beauty. Death like a slow-burning fire is consuming our very hearts. We sense its vital force consuming our ventricles and our aortas, illuminating them, stimulating them, even as it eats them away. Every single beat becomes to us a miracle, one more stay against the final thump before the silence. Desperate for each pulsation of fresh oxygen, we look around, bewildered, until our eyes light on something living to die: a crocus, drooping, or a Maine coon cat. These beings suddenly become to us what they are— self-contained lights, revelations of the quick hum and buzz of life: visions. There they stand, the purplish crocus and the wild-eyed feline.

It is now that we understand the great profundity of the old idea of the *memento mori* (remember that you will die). Meditative souls of the Middle Ages often adorned their tables with skulls or kept close by etchings of skeletons engaged in the danse macabre. Later, during the early

Renaissance, funeral art featured grim reapers or skull and bones. Even later large clocks had engraved upon them mottoes, such as ultima forsan (perhaps the last) or vulnerant omnes, ultima necat (they all wound, and the last kills) or, perhaps the best known, tempus fugit (time flies). Seen in the light of Keats's linkage of melancholy, death, and beauty, these motifs do not appear to be morbid but rather celebratory, vibrant gestures toward life's ambrosial finitude.

When I embrace this theme—and it's extremely difficult to do so—I feel as though my anxiety were an invitation to participate in the great rondure of life. Though my anxiety over death initially makes me feel alone, separated from everything else and forced to face my own unique possibilities, this same feeling eventually encourages me to sense my solidarity with all other living things. I know that we all are this minute, with every new breath, driving toward death. Knowing this, I for an instant penetrate the mysteries of the cosmos's organisms. I sound ambiguous depths. I realize that beneath the surfaces of my very self are the same rhythms that drive the round earth and the stars that seem still. I feel at one with what I can only call Being—beautiful and robust.

Encountering this unity, I feel as though I were authentic, true, alive. All fakeness falls away, and I am at the core of life. This is death's boon, sorrowful yet sonorous, the call to authenticity. What is authenticity but accepting that melancholy death is the muse of my existence, the sweet inspiration that reminds me of who I am and what I can do, that saves me from the masses and keeps me honest? This is indeed authenticity. It is that feeling that my deepest anxieties over passing things makes me who I really am: this unique and unrepeatable possibility, this quivering node of individuality, this miraculous breath of Being. It is further that feeling that this sudden separation from the collective, this delving into my own-most potency, is paradoxically an experience of unity with all organisms, with their sweet contracting and expanding. It, authenticity, is finally that feeling that all of this weird planet, distant yet so intimate, is beautiful in its passing, is so gorgeous, with its desperate starlings and its stark mica, that we want to weep.

IN SEPTEMBER 1787, when Beethoven was but sixteen years old, he revealed a malady that hounded him for the rest of his days. In a letter written soon after the death of his beloved mother, he confessed that he had lately been suffering from grief and from asthma but also from "melancholy," "almost as great an evil" as the other ailments. Long before his deafness, which came on at the turn of the century, Beethoven was already concerned over the discord between himself and the world. This chronic dissatisfaction manifests itself again and again in his letters and his behaviors. This same anxious melancholia also ultimately acted as an inspiration for his symphonic chords.

From the age of sixteen until the age of about thirty, Beethoven created several memorable works. He composed his Trio for Pianoforte (opus 1); his Sonata for Pianoforte (opus 2); his *Moonlight Sonata* (opus 27); his *Pathétique* (opus 14); his Piano Concerto (opus 37); his First and Second

Symphonies; a Quartet for Strings (opus 18); and his ballet, *The Men of Prometheus* (opus 43). However, it wasn't until 1801 that his career ascended to the greatness for which we remember him. This fecund period coincided with one of Beethoven's most melancholy times, a time during which he persistently brooded over his own death and the possibility that it was precisely the onset of his death that might spur him to greater creative heights. Indeed, Beethoven began this period by publishing his first string quartets. The final movement of the last of these six quartets is titled La Malinconia (melancholy). Of another piece written around this time—the largo of opus 10, number 3—Beethoven later wrote: "Everyone at that time sensed [in this work] the mental state of melancholia and its phases, without having a title to provide a key for this."

In June 1801, Beethoven expressed his characteristic melancholia, but with a special intensity. In a letter to a physician friend, he writes that his life, at least on the surface, seems to be going well. His compositions are selling briskly. He enjoys plenty of publishers seeking his work. He has few financial worries. But this appearance hides a cruel reality. Because of his decreased hearing and a pained abdomen, he is prone to "give way to despair." Worried that he will never be healed of his growing deafness and his trouble with the colic, he has "often cursed his Creator and his existence." All that he can cling to now, he claims, is his "resignation." He vows that he will "bid defiance" to his "fate," even though he knows that at times he will be "God's most unhappy creature."

This was the first of many such avowals from Beethoven. In each, he rages against his finitude, claiming that he will overcome his various limitations through creating immortal works. However, even though he clearly hates his inherited troubles—his melancholia, his gastric disorders, his hearing loss—he also acknowledges, though indirectly, that these very constraints are his muse. In rebelling against his "fate" by creating vital music, he actually transforms this same fate into an inspiration. Even though Beethoven does not accept his inevitable decay with as much generosity as does Keats, he nonetheless embodies the same dynamic we witnessed in the British poet: the body's necessary wear, properly seen, gives rise to beauty, gorgeous creations that press against annihilation, that act as negentropic counters to inexorable entropy. Enacting this process, Beethoven both loathes his maladies and embraces them. He hates his condition—it pains him no end—and loves it: it lifts him to the empyrean. This strange situation is ironic, a simultaneous rejection and endorsement, a statement and an antistatement, a setting down and an erasure. Indeed, this is precisely the logic of irony: to mean two things at once, with one thing often being positive and the other negative. That Beethoven is here ironic, as Keats was before him, is curious, since this composer of fantastic passion seems to take everything so seriously. Still, this simultaneous detachment from and attachment to death is an essential dimension of the melancholy life.

Soon after Beethoven vowed to defy his fate with art, thus indirectly promoting this same fate to amuse, he again railed against his illness in such a way that he aggrandized this sickness in spite of himself. In another letter to another friend, Beethoven claims that he is leading a "very unhappy life and is at variance with Nature and his Creator." Because his hearing is deteriorating, he has "cursed [God]" "many times." Beethoven now leads "a sad life," for he is "cut off from everything that is dear and precious" to him. All he has recourse to, he concludes, is "[s]ad resignation." He "is resolved" to overcome his depression, though, but wonders how this is to be done. Some months later he found a way. He vowed in another letter that he "will seize Fate by the throat" and not let it "bend and crush" him completely. He will resist his fate in the only way that he knows how: through frenzied creations that will transcend time, music so miraculous that it can never, not for a minute, die.

Regardless of this ferocious vow, Beethoven again soon sank into a terrible malaise. So bad was his mood that another of his physicians recommended that he retire to the country for a season. He took this advice. In the fall of 1802 he traveled to the small village of Heiligenstadt. There he hoped to convalesce, to recover some of his hearing and to improve his dark moods, moods that had been with him long before his hearing suffered. Sadly the scheme for renewed health didn't work. A friend who visited Beethoven in this village recalled a time when he alerted the great composer to a shepherd "piping very agreeably on a flute made of a twig of elder." Unable to hear clearly, Beethoven became "extremely quiet and morose," a condition that lasted for most of the friend's visit. When Beethoven did on rare occasions attempt to be merry, the friend further reported, "it was generally to the extreme of boisterousness." It was false and strained. This descent into debilitating melancholia reveals the difficulty of maintaining, in the face of terrible sadness, the Keatsian buoyancy, the ability to translate suffering to joy, death to life—time's ravages into unforgettable ravishments.

Indeed, Beethoven expressed his profound melancholia during this period. Still, despite his agony, he continued to find ways to affirm his gloom. In the famous Heiligenstadt confession—a long letter to his two brothers, never sent—Beethoven describes his horrible mental and physical existence with bracing candor. He again laments the state of his hearing, and he blames this condition for his almost total isolation. His increasing deafness has exacerbated his already melancholy temperament and pushed him to despair. So intense is his melancholia that he has thought of ending his life. Only his art, he confesses, has stayed his hand. It seems to him "impossible to leave the world until [he] had brought forth all that [he] felt was within [him]." He vows to endure his "wretched" condition so that he can bring his talent to fruition.

Given Beethoven's terrible melancholy, a mood that had plagued him regardless of his deafness, it is amazing that he was able to compose at all. When we actually view his output around this time, we are absolutely stunned. Around this time Beethoven was reported to have said that "I am not very well satisfied with the work I have thus far done. From this day on I shall take a new way." This is precisely what he did. He moved beyond the classical style of his youth to a strikingly new and avant-garde style, the Romantic style. Here at the outset of what is now known as his heroic age, Beethoven discovered a style capable of expressing the deep, wild emotions of his heart. It produced some of the most emotional compositions in his canon.

Between 1802 and 1810, Beethoven created several of his most unforgettable masterpieces. These great works included the Tempest Sonata (opus 3); the *Eroica*, or Third, Symphony; the Waldheim Sonata (opus 53); his only opera, *Fidelio*; the *Emperor*, or Fifth, Piano Concerto (opus 74); his Fourth Symphony; and his most famous of all symphonies, the Fifth. Each of these works is a stirring and brooding exploration of the melancholy heart. They still cause our souls to shiver, inspiring us to delve into vitally dark places usually beyond our ken.

Though Beethoven of course went on to compose other masterworks—namely, the Ninth Symphony—he never again experienced the creative frenzy of these extremely melancholy years between 1802 and 1810. So stoked was he on the music of the heavenly spheres that he improvised on his pianoforte for hours on end. He scribbled wild musical notations on the shutters and the walls. He often forgot to eat supper. He sometimes poured water over his unwashed head in order to keep awake. Out of this mania grew what Haydn called "things of beauty, but rather dark and strange."

AS I MENTIONED, this relationship among melancholy, death, and beauty is ironic. We must keep in mind that irony need not be mere glibness or sarcasm. Irony can also constitute a wondrous paradox, the ability to be serious and play-ful at once. This paradoxical irony is irony of a special sort, Romantic irony. Different from mere wordplay, this kind of irony unveils yet another aspect of melancholia: the mood fosters an ability to be utterly involved in the suffering world but also, at the same time, out of the game, above the fray, aloof, tranquil, as graceful as the indifferent dawn.

Romantic irony, developed mainly in the late eighteenth and early nineteenth centuries by German philosophers like Friedrich von Schlegel, assumes that the universe is simply too capacious, too overabundant, too complex, ever to be ac-curately represented by any one thought, image, or state-ment. To attempt to squeeze this teeming cosmos into one representation is to be reductive, shallow, small. The only way to reflect the energy of this bursting world is to create concepts or pictures or sentences that somehow exist and don't exist at once, that posit their existence only to erase themselves. Such paradoxical elements highlight the fact that this universe can never be captured in one paradigm. They, these paradoxical events, are simultaneously mean-ingful—they tell us something important about the world—and meaningless: they are nothing compared with this world's infinite significations. They are lucid and dark, vi-sionary and blind.

These self-erasing expressions of the bristling universe can take many forms. They can come in the form of a novel with a self-conscious narrator, a presence that makes it clear that his work is not reality but a fiction, a mere approxima-tion of the real. They can also take the form of an essay divided against itself, a piece that posits one position only to question it later with another position that in turn itself is questioned. These self-consuming artifacts can furthermore be constituted by poems so complexly paradoxical that they contain two diametrically opposed meanings at one time, each of which is equally valid. Finally, these combustible representations can be fragments, incomplete works that highlight the fact that all efforts to reflect the world are ultimately fragmentary.

Though it often organizes literary expression, Romantic irony is basically an attitude, a disposition, a way of being. It is a method for making sense of the world without being dogmatic, for remaining open-minded in the face of inevitable indeterminacy, for being able to remain in an interpretive limbo, aware of the fact that no one perspective on the world is ever finally true. The person who is ironic in this way ultimately takes life seriously and not seriously at the same time. He knows that his experience of the world is dynamic, vital, fascinating. But he also realizes that this same experience is utterly inadequate, incomplete, banal. He has his world and leaves it too.

Romantic irony and melancholia are inseparable. To be melancholy is to live in perpetual doubt, persistent confusion. Such vague bewilderment, properly seen, is not a failure of knowledge. It is rather an honest willingness to accept the fact that we can never know anything once and for all, that we are inevitably ignorant of the whole truth. Accepting this, we must often endure a gloomy limbo. But we are also open to the brisk interplay between life's oppositions and the possibility of understanding, however briefly, the nature of the interplay. Such openness is necessarily ironic, for it never grasps wholeheartedly at one interpretation or another, at one antinomy or another. This open stance is indeed playful, bordering on innocence, fully attuned to possibility, the irreducible ambiguity of experience, the uncertain and bumbling murmurs of time.

Necessarily melancholy, this form of irony is also cognizant of the relationship between death and beauty. Unwilling to embrace one interpretation at the expense of all others, the ironist places himself in perpetual insecurity. Extending into the unknown, he necessarily feels his own inability ever to achieve complete knowledge. He feels fragmented, unfinished, finite. He understands, deep in his heart, this: he will die. Struck by this insight, he suddenly senses a new vitality rise in his veins. He realizes he must make the most of his short and confused time. He must hug the world hard, experience its beauty and create beauty. In this way, this melancholy ironist discovers the relationship articulated by Keats and embodied by Beethoven. On the one hand, the melancholy soul hates death, for it causes him endless turmoil and pain. On the other hand, this same melancholy person embraces death because it inspires him to perceive and to create beauty. Ironically, death is meaningless and meaningful at once.

Fittingly, Keats expresses this form of melancholy irony is one of his most famous letters. In this epistle from 1818, Keats claims that a "Man of Achievement... especially in Literature" must possess *"Negative Capability."* This talent is on display when a person "is capable of being in uncertainties, Mysteries, doubts, without any irritable reaching after fact & reason." This ability requires that one remain unattached from any content position, that one dwell in endless and rich limbo. But it is precisely there that one grows to understand the great energies of the world, always in the middle. For Keats, Shakespeare possessed this capability more than anyone else. We could of course also conclude that Beethoven and Keats exhibited this skill as well.

Perhaps the most memorable characteristic of the works of these two great artists is the lack of controlling ego. When we experience the works of these artists, we are overwhelmed with an overabundance of signification. We simply cannot find the one point of view on which we can settle. We feel as though we were witnessing the fullness of the cosmos. No wonder these works hold numerous and contradictory meanings in the same artistic space. No wonder Keats claims in another letter that the "poetical Character...has no self—it is everything and nothing...it enjoys light and shade."

It should by now be clear this capacious, unselfish melancholy irony is absolutely not the shallow, selfish irony embodied by jaded twenty- and thirty-somethings. Their irony rejects sincerity and richness and tragedy and fullness of any kind. It has seen and done everything ("been there, done that"). It is infected with mockery ("yeah, right"). Likewise, this isn't the kind of irony you see on *Saturday Night Live* or *South Park* or *Family Guy*, parody merely for comedy. Nor is this the irony of the Tarantino sort, which measures hipness by the amount of pop culture you can cite and mimic. Finally, this is not the irony of the *Seinfeld* kind, a form that says that you should take nothing seriously ("no hugging, no learning") but instead should make fun of everything.

Each of these kinds of irony—pervasive among Generation Xers and probably also among Generation Y types—assumes distance. No matter how potentially moving an experience is, I can stand outside it and mock it. I am untouched by anything approaching the real. I stand to the side and comment, but I don't participate. There is an obvious perversity to this, a refusal to engage feeling.

This kind of postmodern irony—let's call it instrumental irony, for it is only a tool wresting us from the present moment—borders on nihilism. How can I value anything at all if I'm constantly extricating myself from concrete situations so that I can snidely comment on the particulars? How can I get any adhesion to life at all if I'm chronically repelling the things that make up my environment? To practice instrumental irony is to choose, rather mindlessly, to become a kind of ghost, a tenuous presence floating around the exquisite pressures of life, all the while whispering apathetic asides on the silliness of it all, on the allegedly empty core of existence.

Perhaps this sort of irony is as much a cause as anything else for the general tolerance for a recent war based largely on fictions concocted by a corrupt administration. Likewise, this same irony is also partially responsible for the almost ubiquitous malaise in the face of the serious civil rights abuses of the Patriot Act. Certainly, the blind patriotism of the happy types largely accounts for the fact that this culture has more or less given this preemptive and power-hungry government a pass. However, the pervasive apathy of the instrumental ironists must be blamed as well. These aloof commentators simply don't care about anything enough to take a difficult stand.

But what about that patriotic sentimentality those happy types love so much? Shouldn't this be mocked? Yes, of course, we'll take irony any day over sentimentality. Still, we must question the glib irony that rules our culture, for it too, like addiction to happiness, divorces one from the real. The ironic poseur, despite all his edginess and neurosis, is entirely detached, unmoored, a denier of blood and guts. He is but a shrugger, a pseudocool faker, an eye roller, a courtier of contempt.

Melancholy irony finds a precarious balance between attachment and detachment. It creates as much as it destroys. It participates in the rhythms of life even as it distances itself from these same rhythms. Sinking into life while removing itself from this same life, this form of irony is transcendent, a way of being in the world and outside the world at once, trapped in time but also above temporality.

Melancholy irony is a serious form of play, a jesting gesture that is dire. As such, this kind of irony connects to the chastened innocence that we noticed earlier. This form of innocence, recall, was not mere simplicity or gullibility. On the contrary, this sort of innocence is attuned to melancholy experience; it grows out of the gloomy limbo and offers a quick repose in the midst of doubt, a sudden vision of a healing third term. By opening one to the vigorous interplay between opposites, irony prepares one for the innocent experience, for that organized innocence that weeps with joy.

IT WAS IN MAY 1968, on the night before his wife Cynthia was set to return from her vacation to Greece, that John Lennon decided to invite an artist to his country home in Weybridge. This artist, a Japanese-born woman named Yoko Ono, had exhibited her work in London's Indica Gallery in 1966, when Lennon was recording *Sgt. Pepper's Lonely Hearts Club Band.* A key player in New York's avant-garde Fluxus movement, a movement partially responsible for inventing performance art, Ono showed in her art a witty intelligence that appealed to Lennon's own quirky mind. For instance, in her Indica exhibition, she featured a work titled *Ceiling Painting.* This piece highlighted a tall silver stepladder elevated on a bright white platform. The ladder rested underneath a suspended white square. Hanging down from the square was a thin chain with a ring at the bottom. This chain resembled the pull on an attic door. The ensemble looked like a ladder standing under a ceiling portal. The wit—the irony—in this piece was rich. The title itself was a pun. It suggested a painting *on* a ceiling and thus recalled the grandeur of Michelangelo. But it also intimated the simple painting *of* a ceiling, therefore invoking images of ordinary housepainters. In this way, the structure paradoxically hinted at both sublime transcendence—a ladder to the heavens— and mere drudgery: backbreaking labor. As such, the piece placed in the conflict the sacred and the profane, the spiritual and the material, illumination and ignorance, with each pole working both to cancel and to intensify its opposite. Having already written two books, *In His Own Write* (1964) and *A Spaniard in the Works* (1965), replete with striking mixtures of high art and low humor, Lennon no doubt appreciated Ono's ironic intelligence in this and other artworks. He likely had that very piece in mind when he invited her to his home on that May evening.

John and Yoko on this night immediately felt a keen attraction to each other. They decided to record their all-night conversation. This recording soon after became their first collaboration, *Unfinished Music No. 1: Two Virgins*. Like the artwork of Yoko and the prose of John, this piece is organized by irony; it is both music and not music at once, a completed album and an incomplete draft, a full object and a fragment. After rapping throughout the darkness, John and Yoko made love at dawn. When Cynthia returned later that afternoon, she saw her husband and his new lover sitting quietly drinking tea. She was startled by their closeness. She knew she had lost John.

John admitted that he knew that other losses, just as painful, were about to come. He felt that Yoko opened in him a side that had been stifled by his work with the Beatles. He realized that he would soon have to break with this group as well. But John was used to pain and sadness and, indeed, constantly transformed this emotional torture into his art. As he said in 1970, just after the Beatles made their last music together, "You're born in pain, and pain is what we're in most of the time. And I think the bigger the pain, the more gods we need." John no doubt based these words on his earliest memories. He was born in Liverpool in 1940 amid the harsh sound of air-raid sirens. He came to consciousness with his father, Alfred, almost always gone to sea. Eventually John's mother, Julia, became weary of the long absences. While her husband was away, she became pregnant by another man. When Alfred returned, he tried to keep his family together but failed. He told young John that he would have to choose between his dad and his mom. John picked his mom but was almost immediately abandoned by her. He was largely raised by his aunt Mimi, even though he craved his mother's presence. His loss of a mother was tragically doubled in 1958, when a car driven by an off-duty drunken policemen hit and killed Julia. As John confessed in 1980, "I lost her twice. Once as a five year old when I moved in with my auntie. And once again ... when she actually physically died ... The underlying chip I had on my shoulder as a youth got really big then. Being a teenager and a rock & roller and an art student and my mother being killed just when I was re-establishing my relationship with her ... was very traumatic for me." These losses and their attendant melancholia haunted John his entire life, especially informing his early solo work and his persistently mordant wit.

Out of John's painful splits—with his father, his mother, his first wife, Cynthia, the Beatles—grew his hunger to create holy art, filled with the gods of the tortured heart. Soon after he and Yoko had released their first album, which is also, ironically, not an album, they followed with yet another witty parody of the traditional disk, *Unfinished Music 2: Life with the Lions.* Part of this record featured Yoko and John crying out to each other while Yoko was in the hospital giving birth to their son, Sean. This playfulness later translated into unforgettable antics, a kind of performance art, of John and Yoko: the famous "bed-in" in Amsterdam, in which the two said they'd remain in bed until the war in Vietnam ended; the "lie-in" for peace in Montreal, in which they, along with several friends, recorded "Give Peace a Chance" in a hotel room; John's public return, with Yoko's support, of his MBE card to the queen, along with a letter that went like this: "Your Majesty, I am returning this in protest against Britain's involvement in the Nigeria-Biafra thing, against our support of America in Vietnam, and against Cold Turkey slipping down the charts. With love. John Lennon of Bag."

Such acts of droll irony—simultaneous endorsements and parodies of be-ins, love-ins, and protest letters—translated in 1970 into one of John and Yoko's most powerful productions, the album *John Lennon/Plastic Ono Band.* Gone is the purely playful irony of the first two albums and the various performance gigs. In its place is a more serious irony, centered on this paradox: the music is both desperately ugly—it constitutes a long, primal melancholy scream of pain—and powerfully melodic; it is a transformation of the scream into transcendent intonations. During this time John was undergoing a form of psychotherapeutic treatment created by the psychologist Arthur Janov. The idea behind this therapy was that the patient needs to return to his deepest repressed pains and purge them through extreme screaming.

Pained over his numerous losses, John found this therapy effective, and he turned his deep wailing into his music. This guttural intoning, a kind of music and nonmusic, a sort of meaningful sound that is meaningless, is especially present in famous songs like "Mother," "Isolation," and "I Found Out." But this ironic method reaches its full power in what the *Rolling Stone* writer Mikal Gilmore calls the album's "crowning achievement," a song titled, simply and terrifyingly, "God." After invoking and rejecting various forms of myth and history, John at the end of the song, in a voice pervaded with pain, confesses even that he no longer believes in his old rock band, the Beatles. He believes only in himself and Yoko. His relationship with her is the only reality, he concludes. Indeed, all dreams of meaning must be stripped away. While John was earlier the weaver of such dreams, he is now simply a man reborn into his new reality. In this new identity, he can no longer provide comforting visions for his listeners, as he did when he was a Beatle. His fans will have to proceed on their own. These sentiments, rendered in that paradoxical merging of screaming and sonorousness, suggest that no one belief system can bear an unfathomable reality. To find any truth, one must reject all easy systems and stand unadorned before the universe and make oneself, through love, vulnerable to another. This mystery of love is ultimately beyond words and can be best expressed, like the pain of primal loss, in musically unmusical wailing.

Whether serious or playful, John Lennon, with the aid of his partner Yoko Ono, remains one of the great melancholy ironists of our recent time. Like Bob Dylan, he continually played the sorrowful trickster, the figure constantly eluding easy categorization. Just when the world thought it had Lennon pegged, he would renounce his old way of doing things and come up with a new gig. This constant changing was not idle contrariness. Instead, this endless transformation grew out of an attunement to the ever-changing and superabundant universe. In a cosmos that cannot be described by any one concept, the best way to move with the grain of nature is to play with forms, to embrace them only to reject them. In this way, one remains free of hang-ups, predictable fixations, stifling habits. While such work is necessarily melancholy—it can never rest in comfortable happiness—it is also exhilarating: participation, almost mystical, in the persistently antithetical structures of the polarized universe.

LENNON'S DEVELOPMENT of melancholy irony, like that of Keats and Beethoven before him, puts another spin on the idea of dynamic innocence that we earlier explored. We now realize that this kind of innocence, growing from sadness and momentarily relieving the sorrow, emerges from irony and that it is also, necessarily, aesthetic. Melancholy irony— Romantic irony—is the ability to play among various forms without becoming overly attached to any one form. In this way, this kind of irony, gloomy in its persistent insecurity yet bracing in its constant vitality, is capable of vacillating back and forth between the earth's polarities, of dwelling for long periods in the rich limbo of the between. Thriving in the middle, this irony inevitably longs for a vision of brisk union between the antinomies, an innocent witness of tense concord. This concord is always a moment of beauty, a time when life is energized by death, and death animated by life.

The great theoretician of this connection among innocence, irony, and beauty is a contemporary of Schlegel's. He is Friedrich von Schiller. In *Letters on the Aesthetic Education of Man* (1795), Schiller claims we all are melancholy. We are this way because of the fall from simple innocence. We are no longer purely at home with ourselves. We are self-conscious, infected with striving. Specifically, we are torn between a drive toward transience, the flow of matter, and a push toward form, stable abstraction.

In some moods, we are in love with the flux of time. We can accept the fact that the world grows and decays, that its weird kiwis and bizarre rhizomes are thrown into the cosmos and then out again, in a blink. In fact, we enjoy simply moving with the flux, with the waxing and the waning, the quick and the dead. We know that we are going to die, and we will it so, for we know that this very death is a spur to vital living.

But this mood is never untroubled. We know that it, like everything else, will pass, is indeed already passing. We lament this ephemerality. We wish that some things—the things we love (the sniffling kiwi and the rhizome underground)—would stay behind, would, for once, stop, and for good. We hunger for permanence in the change, a beauty that will stand firm in the flow, an indelible snapshot, luminous and sharp.

Feeling the earth slip precipitously between our fingers, we turn to another mood. We come to adore form. We search for ideas and works, for philosophies and poems, that stand above the ravages and wrecks of time. We begin to feel deep attraction to stasis, to notions of eternity. We ignore the concrete cosmos, with all its corpses, and cultivate instead abstraction, stable concepts with no need for grunting anatomies.

However, this mood too grows troublous. We understand that stasis is lifeless, an analogy to death itself. We before long regret our fixation on form. We want once again to jump into the fray, to caress soft fur and dig for labyrinthine roots. We yearn for blood and circulation, for motion and quivering and quaking.

But then once more we want the permanence, and then again we desire the change. This process feels never-ending, as though we were doomed to vacillate between opposing poles. This is our fallen condition, our melancholy situation. If we are authentic, we seldom find rest in the midst of this back-and-forth game. We often become exhausted by the jostling. We desire some respite from the persistent division.

The only way to achieve this respite is through playful irony. We must understand that neither energy nor form is sufficient unto itself. One needs the other to become meaningful. Energy without form is chaotic flux, a calamitous drive toward violent death. Form without energy is numb stasis, an eternal state of quiet death. However, energy with an eye toward form gains a tenuous rectitude, a vague order. Form with attention to energy becomes vital, a pattern of turbulence.

LEST WE right here think that too much has been claimed for melancholia—that the gloomy disposition surely can't be a spur for such playful possibilities—we must quickly recall Handel, the composer of the eighteenth century. By 1741, when he was in his mid-fifties, Handel found himself a fallen man. Once a ruler of the musical world, he for a litany of reasons had descended into terrible poverty, awful health, and deep depression. Living in a run-down house in a poor part of London, he expected any day to be thrown into debtor's prison or to die. But then, out of nowhere, as if by some divine agency, Handel received a libretto based on the life of Jesus and an invitation to compose a work for a charity benefit performance. On August 22, 1741, in his squalid rooms on Brook Street, Handel saw potentialities no one had before seen. He began to work. Immediately he felt a creative energy course through his veins: an energy that appeared to come from heaven itself. During a twenty-four-day period he barely slept or ate. He only composed, and then composed more. At the close of this brief season he had completed *The Messiah*, his greatest work, a gift from the depths of melancholia.

We might also remember in this context Virginia Woolf. Her two greatest works, *Mrs. Dalloway* (1925) and *To the Lighthouse* (1927), feature the shockingly gorgeous interiors of nostalgic souls. Out of these characters' yearnings grows exquisite insights into the mysteries of self and the universe. These novels had their birth in the agitated womb of Woolf's chronic melancholia. Woolf was often terrified by fits of real madness, a madness that led to her suicide. However, she nonetheless lauded her nervous melancholia as her most powerful inspiration. As she wrote around 1913, "As an experience, madness is terrific . . . and not to be sniffed at, and in its lava I still find most of the things I write about. It shoots out of one everything—shaped, final, not in mere driblets as sanity does." At another time she claimed that her gloomy periods, heavy counters to her nervous times, were desirable, regardless of their horrific character: "But it is always a question whether I wish to avoid these glooms," during which she "goes down into the well" where nothing protects her "from the assault of truth." In either case—whether she be stoked by frenzy or slowed by sorrow—Woolf viewed her melancholia, dangerous though it was, as a source of violent truth and smoldering creation.

We might even at this juncture do well to recall the case of Georgia O'Keeffe, the artist of the first part of the twentieth century. In the late 1920s and early '30s, O'Keeffe left the East Coast and traveled to Taos, New Mexico. She fell profoundly in love with the lonely vistas of this world denuded of human corruption. However, even though she was enlivened by this part of the world, in 1932 her lifelong battle with melancholia caught up with her. She was hospitalized for psychoneurosis. Rather than quell her creative spirit, this breakdown did the opposite. Upon being discharged, she wrote to an intimate: "I am not sick anymore. Everything in me begins to move." She returned to the Southwest. There in 1935 she painted some of her bleakest and most beautiful landscapes: *Hills near Abiqui* and *Ram's Head, White Hollyhock-Hills*. Both feature dark things amid the bright desert, gloomy shadows and stormy clouds. Into these haunting shades, hovering amid hardscrabble rock and a sinister skull, one stares. In these depths one senses something as silent and holy as bones.

These brief vignettes—and there are hundreds of others I could have chosen—confirm what I have continued to suggest: melancholia, far from a mere disease or weakness of will, is an almost miraculous invitation to transcend the banal status quo and imagine the untapped possibilities for existence. Without melancholia, the earth would likely freeze over into a fixed state, as predictable as metal. Only with the help of constant sorrow can this dying world be changed, enlivened, pushed to the new.

These are not metaphysical claims, not some New Age claptrap. On the contrary, these statements are attuned to the sloppy world as it simply appears to us in our everyday experience. When we with apparent happiness grab hard onto one ideology or another, this world suddenly seems to take on a static coherence, a rigid division between right and wrong. The world in this way becomes uninteresting, dead. But when we allow our melancholy mood to bloom in our hearts, this universe, formerly inanimate, comes suddenly to life. Finite rules dissolve before infinite possibilities. Green things, in abundance, grow, constituting a potent plethora. Now happiness to us is no longer viable. We want something more, joy. And we know that this can come only through the humming corridors of melancholia, that irony, galvanizing, shocks us to life.

This is indeed the greatest irony of all: the true path to ecstatic joy is through acute melancholia. To take a stance against American happiness—tepid satisfaction—is to stand close to extreme jubilance, rapturous abandonment. The surest way to suffer what Thoreau calls "quiet desperation" is to try to lead the perfectly happy American life. Attempting this, you will always be dissatisfied, for you are repressing that rich darkness of the soul. Allowing this creative gloom into the light, you inexorably move away from the silent worry to Thoreau's most cherished state, wildness. As Thoreau memorably put it, our "village life would stagnate if it were not for the unexplored forests and the meadows which surround it. We need the tonic of wildness—to wade sometimes in marshes where the bittern and the meadow-hen lurk, and hear the booming of the snipe; to smell the whispering hedge where only some wilder and more solitary fowl builds her nest, and the mink crawls with its belly close to the ground."

CONCLUSION

Whoever commits to paper what he suffers becomes
a melancholy author: but he becomes a serious
author when he tells us what he suffered and why
he now reposes in joy.
—FRIEDRICH NIETZSCHE

THE GENE POOL—before and beyond time—froths and sloshes. What flops up onto the temporal shores is a matter of chance, a product of the waves' whims. At some point this teeming reservoir of DNA spumes forth a saturnine gene, a double helix destined to produce melancholy dispositions. From this instant onward what we know as human history begins: that striving, seemingly endless, toward an ungraspable perfection, that tragic effort to reach what exceeds the grasp, to fail magnificently. This gene, this melancholy gene, has proved the code for innovation. It has produced over the centuries our resplendent towers, yearning heavenward. It has created our great epics, god-hungry.

It has concocted our memorable symphonies, as tumultuously beautiful as the first ocean. Without this sorrowful genome, these sublimities would have remained in the netherworld of nonexistence. Indeed, without this genetic information, sullen and ambitious, what we see as culture in general, that empyreal realm of straining ideas, might have never arisen from the mere quest for survival, from simple killing and eating.

We can picture this in the primitive world. While the healthy bodies of the tribe were out mindlessly hacking beasts or other humans, the melancholy soul remained behind brooding in a cave or under a tree. There he imagined new structures, oval and amber, or fresh verbal rhythms, sacred summonings, or songs superior to even those of the birds. Envisioning these things, and more, this melancholy malingerer became just as useful for his culture as did the hunters and the gatherers for theirs. He pushed his world ahead. He moved it forward. He dwelled always in the insecure realm of the avant-garde.

This primitive visionary was the first of many such avant-garde melancholics. Of course not all innovators are melancholy, and not all melancholy souls are innovative. However, the scientifically proved relationship between genius and depression, between gloom and greatness suggests that the majority of our cultural innovators, ranging from the ancient dreamer in the bush to the more recent Dadaist in the city, have grounded their originality in the melancholy mood. We can of course by now understand why.

Melancholia pushes against the easy "either/or" of the

status quo. It thrives in unexplored middle ground between oppositions, in the "both/and." It fosters fresh insights into relationships between oppositions, especially that great polarity life and death. It encourages new ways of conceiving and naming the mysterious connections between antinomies. It returns us to innocence, to irony, that ability, temporary, to play in potential without being constrained to the actual. Such respites from causality refresh our relationship to the world, grant us beautiful vistas, energize our hearts and our minds.

Indeed, the world is much of the time boring, controlled as it is by staid habits. It seems overly familiar, tired, repetitious. Then along comes what Keats calls the melancholy fit, and suddenly the planet again turns interesting. The veil of familiarity falls away. There before us flare bracing possibilities. We are called to forge untested links to our environments. We are summoned to be creative.

Given these virtues of melancholia, why are thousands of psychiatrists and psychologists attempting to "cure" depression as if it were a terrible disease? Obviously, those suffering severe depression, suicidal and bordering on psychosis, require serious medications. But what of those millions of people who possess mild to moderate depression? Should these potential visionaries also be asked to eradicate their melancholia with the help of a pill? Should these possible innovators relinquish what might well be their greatest muse, their demons giving birth to angels?

Right now, if the statistics are correct, about 15 percent of Americans are not happy. Soon, perhaps, with the help of psychopharmaceuticals, we shall have no more unhappy people in our country. Melancholics will become unknown.

This would be an unparalleled tragedy, equivalent in scope to the annihilation of the sperm whale or the golden eagle. With no more melancholics, we would live in a world in which everyone simply accepted the status quo, in which everyone would simply be content with the given. This would constitute a dystopia of ubiquitous placid grins, a nightmare worthy of Philip K. Dick, a police state of Pollyannas, a flatland that offers nothing new under the sun. Why are we pushing toward such a hellish condition?

The answer is simple: fear. Most hide behind the smile because they are afraid of facing the world's complexity, its vagueness, its terrible beauties. If they stay safely ensconced behind their painted grins, then they won't have to encounter the insecurities attendant upon dwelling in possibility, those anxious moments when one doesn't know this from that, when one could suddenly become almost anything at all. Even though this anxiety, usually over death, is in the end exhilarating, a call to be creative, it is in the beginning rather horrifying, a feeling of hovering in an unpredictable abyss. Most immediately flee from this situation. They try to lose themselves in the laughing masses, hoping the anxiety will never again visit them. They don inauthenticity as a mask, a disguise protecting them from the abyss.

To foster a society of total happiness is to concoct a culture of fear. Do we really want to give away our courage for mere mirth? Are we ready to relinquish our most essential hearts for a good night's sleep, a season of contentment? We must ignore the seductions of our blissed-out culture and somehow hold to our sadness. We must find a way, difficult though it is, to be who we are, sullenness and all.

Suffering the gloom, inevitable as breath, we must further accept this fact that the world hates: we are forever incomplete, but fragments of some ungraspable whole. Our unfinished natures—we are never pure actualities but always vague potentials—make life a constant struggle, a bout with the persistent unknown. But this extension into the abyss is also our salvation. To be but a fragment is always to strive for something beyond oneself, something transcendent—an unexplored possibility, an unmapped avenue. This striving is always an act of freedom, of choosing one road instead of another. Though this labor is arduous—it requires constant attention to our mysterious and shifting interiors—it is also ecstatic, an almost infinite sounding of the exquisite riddles of Being.

To be against happiness, to avert contentment, is to be close to joy, to embrace ecstasy. Incompleteness is the call to life. Fragmentation is freedom. The exhilaration of never knowing anything fully is that you can perpetually imagine sublimities beyond reason. On the margins of the known is the agile edge of existence. This is the elation of circumference. This is the rapture, burning slow, of finishing a book that can never be completed, a flawed and conflicted text, vexed as twilight.

Bibliographical Notes

INTRODUCTION

I was first led to consider the relationship between melancholia and evolution by two excellent books: Kay Redfield Jamison's *Touched by Fire: Manic Depressive Illness and the Artistic Temperament* (New York: Free Press, 1996) and Daniel Nettle's *Strong Imagination: Madness, Creativity, and Human Nature* (New York and Oxford, U.K.: Oxford University Press, 2001). I mainly base my meditations in this introduction on the Pew Research Center's Social Trends report titled *Are We Happy Yet?* Compiled by Paul Taylor, Cary Funk, and Peyton Craighill, this examines the results of several surveys related to American happiness. A convenient summary of the report's results can be found on the Pew Research Center's website, pewresearch.org/pubs/301/are-we-happy-yet. Michael Powell has published a revealing article on this study in *The Washington Post*: "A Study Finds Americans Unrelentingly Cheerful," February 14, 2006, p. A02. I also ground my ideas in this chapter on the new trend in psychology, positive psychology, founded by Dr. Martin Seligman. The director of the University of Pennsylvania Psychology Center, Seligman has developed a program designed to enhance happiness. He emphasizes the importance of three "domains" of happiness: a pleasant life, an engaged life, and a meaningful life. Seligman's most important work, the seminal work in the field, is *Authentic Happiness: Using the New Positive Psychology to Realize Your Potential for Lasting Fulfillment* (New York: Free Press, 2004). The January 2005 issue of *Time* magazine is devoted entirely to this new trend. See especially Claudia Wills's "The New Science of Happiness." Beginning on April 30, 2006, the BBC aired a six-part series on this new sort of psychology. The October 2, 2005, edition of *The New York Times Magazine* did a full spread on the trend. Cecilia Capuzzi Simon penned an informative *Washington Post* article on the subject: "The Happy Heretic: Martin Seligman Thinks Psychologists Should Help People Be Happy. Who Could Possibly Have a Problem with That?" December 24, 2002, p. HE01. Other important figures in the positive psychology movement are Jonathan Haidt (see his *The Happiness Hypothesis: Finding Modern Truth in Ancient Wisdom* [New York: Basic Books, 2006]) and Tal Ben-Shahar (see his *Happier: Secrets to Daily Joy and Lasting Fulfillment* [New York: McGraw-Hill, 2007]). Yet another influence on my ideas in this section is the trend championed by Peter Kramer. In *Against Depression* (New York: Viking, 2005), Kramer argues that depression in any form—even in its creative, melancholy form—is a disease that should be eradicated with proper medicines. He intimates that there might be a time when depression will exist no more. Other books that helped me immensely in framing my arguments are Joshua Wolf Shenk's *Lincoln's Melancholy: How Depression Challenged a President and Fueled His Greatness* (New York: Houghton Mifflin, 2005) and Darrin M. McMahon's *Happiness: A History* (New York: Grove Press, 2006). Both books are intelligent, erudite meditations on the place of sadness in Western culture. Still other influences on my ideas are two recent books that explore the power of melancholy in relation to spiritual growth. One is Thomas Moore's *Dark Nights of the Soul: A Guide to Finding Your Way Through Life's Ordeals* (New York: Gotham, 2004); the other is Gerald G. May's *The Dark Night of the Soul: A Psychiatrist Explores the Connection Between Darkness and Spiritual Growth* (San Francisco: HarperSanFrancisco, 2005). My book is similar to these two in meditating on the virtues of melancholia; my book differs, however, in attacking the vices of happiness. Yet another influence on this chapter, and, indeed, on this entire book, is Ronald W. Dworkin's *Artificial Happiness: The Dark Side of the New Happy Class* (New York: Carroll & Graf, 2006). This book convincingly argues that many doctors now unnecessarily prescribe antidepressants and thus hinder patients from working through their sadness. Dworkin's book is excellent; it is in many ways a physician's version of my more humanistic meditation on the problems of pursuing superficial happiness. Finally, a profound influence on this

book is the work of James Hillman, who has argued for years that depression is necessary for the growth of the soul. See, for instance, Hillman's *Archetypal Psychology* (Dallas, Tex.: Spring Publications, 2004) and
Re-Visioning Psychology (New York: Harper, 1978). The phrase "terrible
beauty" is inspired by W. B. Yeats's poem "Easter, 1916."

THE AMERICAN DREAM

I take William Bradford's words from his famous work, *Of Plymouth Plan-
tation*, ed. and intro. Harvey Wish (New York: Capricorn, 1962), pp.
60–61. For a good recent account of how the Pilgrims, regardless of their
palpable pain and heartbreak, still believed in God's ultimately benevo-
lent providence, see Nathaniel Philbrick's *Mayflower: A Story of Courage,
Community, and War* (New York: Penguin, 2007). For a magisterial study
of Bradford's basic Puritan theology, see Perry Miller's *The New England
Mind: The Seventeenth Century* (Cambridge, Mass., and London: Belknap
Press of Harvard University Press, 1939). For a compact study of the
same, see Edmund S. Morgan's *Visible Saints: The History of a Puritan Idea*
(Ithaca, N.Y., and London: Cornell University Press, 1963). A good edition of Benjamin Franklin's *The Way to Wealth*, written in the persona of
Poor Richard, is *The Way to Wealth* (Carlisle, Mass.: Applewood Books,
2001). For a study of America's move from a religious to a secular state,
see Perry Miller's *The New England Mind: From Colony to Province* (Cambridge, Mass.: Harvard University Press, 1953). A great study of the intellectual background of the Declaration of Independence is Garry Wills's
Inventing America: Jefferson's Declaration of Independence (New York: Mariner
Books of Houghton Mifflin, 2002). For John Locke's political ideas, see
his *Second Treatise of Civil Government* (Amherst, N.Y.: Prometheus Books,
1986). A powerful study of how capitalism fosters loss of the real is Frederick Jameson's *Postmodernism: or, The Cultural Logic of Late Capitalism*
(Durham, N.C.: Duke University Press, 1991). Another seminal study of
this problem is Walter Benjamin's "The Work of Art in the Age of
Mechanical Production" (1936). This piece can be found in Benjamin's
Illuminations, ed. Hannah Arendt and trans. Harry Zohn (New York:
Schocken Books, 1969). The major current in this chapter—that the
quest for happiness at the expense of sadness leads to a one-sided life—
is profoundly expressed in Ralph Waldo Emerson's 1844 essay "Experience." See *Emerson: Selected Essays*, ed. Larzer Ziff (New York: Penguin,

1982), pp. 285–312. The quotation on "the clangor and jangle of contrary tendencies" comes from p. 296. Another major influence on my sense that the desire for joy without pain enervates existence is William Blake's 1794 poem *The Book of Urizen*. See *The Complete Poetry and Prose of William Blake*, ed. David V. Erdman and comm. Harold Bloom (New York: Anchor Books, 1988), pp. 70–83; the quotation on the "solid without fluctuation" and the "joy without pain" comes from p. 71. Blake goes on to say that the only way to experience existence as it is—"infinite"—is to renounce the egotistical desire to gain total and contented control of the world. He makes this claim in "There Is No Natural Religion," pp. 2–3, in *The Complete Poetry and Prose*. Alan W. Watts makes a similar point in his brilliant *The Wisdom of Insecurity: A Message for an Age of Anxiety* (New York: Vintage Books, 1951). See especially the pages from which I quote in the chapter: pp. 77 (the "momentariness" quotation) and 32 (the "lovable" quotation). The idea that happy people are more likely to be bigoted than sad people, found in *Psychological Science*, is reported in a 2004 *New York Times* article by Jim Holt: "The Way We Live Now: Against Happiness," June 4, 2004. The Pew Research Center's report *Are We Happy Yet?* states that Republicans tend to be happier than Democrats. Hawthorne's striking description of Melville's state of mind when he was on his way to Egypt can be found in Jay Leyda's *The Melville Log*, vol. 2 (New York: Gordian Press, 1951), p. 529. Melville's *Moby-Dick* is a profound meditation on the virtues of melancholy. The many quotations that I invoke in this chapter can be found in *Moby-Dick; or, The Whale* (New York: Bantam Classics, 1981), pp. 73, 120, 392. My vignette on Bruce Springsteen's making of "Nebraska" is a somewhat imaginative description of what might have happened in that Colts Neck, New Jersey, house back in late December 1981. I was helped along by Eric Alterman's *It Ain't No Sin to Be Glad You're Alive: The Promise of Bruce Springsteen* (New York: Little, Brown, 1999), pp. 128–31. Alterman also discusses Springsteen's experiences with psychotherapy (pp. 203–204). Springsteen's quotation on how agitated people are more interesting than comfortable ones comes from a DVD included in the packaging for the CD *Devils and Dust*, released by Sony in 2005.

THE MAN OF SORROWS

My brief meditation here on the relationship among anxiety, alienation, and finitude is developed in Martin Heidegger's *Being and Time*, trans. John Macquarrie and Edward Robinson (New York: Harper, 1962), pp. 210–14, 279–311. (Of course one of the great ironies in the history of philosophy is that Heidegger, the great proponent of immediate perception, could fall victim to the violent abstractions of the Nazi Party. It is deeply troubling that a thinker of Heidegger's stature could have such a sinister heart.) A fascinating book on how melancholy relates to our senses of particular things, such as our volumes of, say, Proust, is Peter Schwenger's *The Tears of Things: Melancholy and Physical Objects* (London and Minneapolis: University of Minnesota Press, 2006). Robert Herrick's poem "To the Virgins, to Make Much of Time" can be found in *Robert Herrick*, ed. Douglas Brooks-Davies (New York: Everyman's Library, 1997), p. 30. Walt Whitman's poem "Out of the Cradle Endlessly Rocking" can be found in *Leaves of Grass*, rev. ed., ed. Michael Moon, Sculley Bradley, and Harold W. Blodgett (New York: Norton, 2002), pp. 206–11. Jesus' struggle in the Garden of Gethsemane is described in Matthew 26:36–46. Jesus' fear that his father has forsaken him is reported in Matthew 27:46. Carl Jung reports his excitement over receiving Richard Wilhelm's *The Secret of the Golden Flower* in *Memories, Dream, Reflections*, rec. and ed. Aniela Jaffe (New York: Pantheon, 1961), pp. 197–98. See also Ronald Hayman's description of Jung's excitement in *A Life of Jung* (New York: Norton, 1999), pp. 283–89. For Jung's own detailing of how the book meshed with his own psychoanalytical ideas, see his commentary on *The Secret of the Golden Flower* in *The Secret of the Golden Flower: A Chinese Book of Life*, trans. and expl. Richard Wilhelm, comm. C. G. Jung (New York: Harvest, 1962), pp. 81–137. For a description of Jung's dark period, see his *Memories, Dreams, Reflections*, pp. 170–200. The quotation on the "monstrous flood" comes from *Memories*, p. 175. The quotation on neurosis as a shaper of identity comes from *The Essential Jung*, sel. and intro. Anthony Storr (Princeton, N.J.: Princeton University Press, 1983), p. 152. For Jung's encounters with alchemy, see his *Psychology and Alchemy*, trans. R.F.C. Hull (Princeton, N.J.: Princeton University Press, 1967) and his *Alchemical Studies*, trans. R.F.C. Hull (Princeton, N.J.: Princeton University Press, 1983). In both these books, Jung inflects ideas of the Christ through alchemical grids. For

Jung's most extensive discussion of the Christ in relation to his depth psychology, see his *Aion: Researches into the Phenomenology of the Self*, 2nd ed., trans. R.F.C. Hull (Princeton, N.J.: Princeton University Press, 1959). Norman Vincent Peale's basic philosophy can be found in his 1952 *The Power of Positive Thinking* (New York: Fireside, 2007). The affirmation I quote can be found on p. 99 of that book. Billy Graham's fundamental worldview is given voice in *Troubled Heart: Finding God in the Midst of Pain* (Nashville, Tenn.: Thomas Nelson Press, 1991). In my discussion, I draw especially from pp. 52–54 and pp. 168–74. Grünwald's *The Crucifixion* (1515) is a panel from the Isenheim altarpiece; it can be found in the Musée d'Unterlinden, Colmar, France. For St. John's *The Dark Night of the Soul*, see the Dover edition from 2003. Dalí's *Christ of St. John of the Cross* (1951) can be found in Glasgow, Scotland's Kelvingrove Art Gallery. The best biography of Blake is Peter Ackroyd's *Blake* (New York: Vintage, 1996). Blake's quotation on the vices of generalization and the virtues of attending to the particular can be found in *The Complete Poetry and Prose of William Blake* (cited above), p. 641. The quotation on the particular being sublime can likewise be found in this text, p. 647. My remarks on Blake's senses of the concrete are largely informed by Northrop Frye's still-brilliant study *Fearful Symmetry: A Study of William Blake* (Princeton, N.J.: Princeton University Press, 1947), pp. 3–30. The quotation on the "doors of perception" can be found in *The Complete Poetry and Prose*, p. 39. Blake expresses the idea that abstract "Philosophical and Experimental" perception reduces experience to repetition in "There Is No Natural Religion" (1788) (*The Complete Poetry and Prose*, pp. 2–3). My remarks on eternity and infinity have been influenced by Frye's *Fearful Symmetry*, pp. 45–48. Blake's comment on Lavatar can be found in *The Complete Poetry and Prose*, p. 601. Blake's phrase "mind-forg'd manacles" comes from his poem "London," part of his *Songs of Experience*.

GENERATIVE MELANCHOLIA

A very helpful work on Marsilio Ficino is *Marsilio Ficino: His Theology, His Philosophy, His Legacy*, ed. Michael J. B. Allen, Valery Rees, and Martin Davies (Boston and Leiden, Neth.: Brill Academic Publishers, 2001). Other essential works on Ficino and the tradition of meditative melancholy are Frances A. Yates's *Giordano Bruno and the Hermetic Tradition* (Chicago and London: University of Chicago Press, 1964) and *The Occult*

Philosophy in the Elizabethan Age (London and New York: Routledge, 1979). Ficino's masterwork is of course *The Book of Life*, trans. Charles Boer (Irving, Tex.: Spring Publications, 1980). A great history of Western melancholia is Raymond Klibansky, Edwin Panofsky, and Fritz Saxl's *Saturn and Melancholy: Studies in the History of Philosophy, Religion, and Art* (New York: Basic Books, 1974). Yates's books are also helpful in this regard, as are *The Nature of Melancholy: From Aristotle to Kristeva*, ed. Jennifer Radden (New York: Oxford, 2002); Jeffrey Smith's *Where Roots Reach for Water: A Personal and Natural History of Melancholy* (New York: North Point Press, 2001); and Andrew Solomon's *The Noonday Demon: An Atlas of Depression* (New York: Scribner, 2002). The quotation from Galen comes from Radden, p. 68. The quotation from Pseudo-Aristotle's *Problems* as well as an astute discussion of the passage comes from *Saturn and Melancholy*, pp. 15–41. Another insightful discussion of the passage from *Problems* can be found in Julia Kristeva's *The Black Sun: Depression and Melancholia*, trans. Leon S. Roudiez (New York: Columbia University Press, 1992), pp. 6–9. Ficino's meditations on this passage and his theory of scholarly melancholy in general can be found in *The Book of Life*, pp. 6–8. The quotation on how the thinker becomes obsessed with "bodiless truths" and thus becomes a "half soul" can be found on p. 7 of Ficino's book. Blake's quote on organized innocence comes from *The Complete Poetry and Prose of William Blake* (cited above), pp. 697, 838. S. Foster Damon's lines can be found in *A Blake Dictionary: The Ideas and Symbols of William Blake*, rev. ed., foreword Morris Eaves (Hanover and London: University Press of New England, 1988), p. 197. Emily Dickinson's poem on "possibility" can be found in *The Poems of Emily Dickinson: Reading Edition* (Cambridge, Mass.: Belknap Press of Harvard University Press, 2005), p. 466. A detailed discussion of Coleridge's limbo can be found in my *Coleridge's Melancholia: An Anatomy of Limbo* (Gainesville: University Press of Florida, 2004). For other excellent books on Coleridge's generative paralyses, see Seamus Perry's *Coleridge and the Uses of Division* (Oxford, U.K.: Oxford University Press, 1999) and Richard Holmes's *Coleridge: Darker Reflections, 1804–1834* (New York: Pantheon, 1998). The quotation on Coleridge's "Degradation" can be found in the *Notebooks of Samuel Taylor Coleridge*, ed. Kathleen Coburn, 5 vols. (New York: Pantheon/Princeton University Press, 1957–2002), vol. 2, p. 2557. The quotation on looking up to the sky and finding no comfort comes from *Notebooks*, vol. 3, p. 4294. The quotation on Coleridge as a gasping fish comes from *Notebooks*, vol. 2, p. 2606. The quotation on the brass candlestick comes from *Note-books*, vol. 2, pp. 713–14. The quotation on paradise and the flower exists in *Notebooks*, vol. 3, p. 4287. I found information on Joni Mitchell's child-hood in Cameron Crowe's "Joni Mitchell," *Rolling Stone* (July 26, 1979). Mitchell's quotation on how bad fortune turned her into a musician ap-pears in the wonderful 2003 PBS documentary *A Woman of Heart and Mind: The Life and Times of Joni Mitchell*, directed by Stephanie Bennett and Susan Lacy and released by Independent Artists. Mitchell's quota-tion on her feeling as transparent as a cellophane wrapper appears in the Cameron Crowe interview cited above. Joni Mitchell's *Blue* is the most powerful manifestation of her melancholy genius. The album was re-leased by Warner Brothers in 1971. Mitchell's lines on how sadness is the "sand that makes the pearl" as well as on how angels and demons go hand in hand can be found in the Bennett-Lacy documentary. Tolstoy's famous quotation on the monotony of happiness can be found in the first line of *Anna Karenina*. Alan Watts's phrase "irreducible rascality" can be found many places throughout his work. The quotation shows up in a lecture titled "The Relevance of Oriental Philosophy" (1973), from a broadcast on New York City's WFMU in 2000. Many have studied the connections between depression and creativity. See mainly Jamison's *Touched by Fire* (cited above); Nettle's *Strong Imagination* (cited above); and D. Jablow Hershman and Julian Lieb's *Manic Depression and Creativity* (Amherst, N.Y.: Prometheus Press, 1998); A revealing portrait of Vincent van Gogh is Albert J. Lubin's *Stranger on Earth: A Psychological Biography of Vincent van Gogh* (New York: Da Capo, 1996). The definitive biography of Hart Crane is John Unterecker's *Voyager: A Life of Hart Crane* (New York: Farrar, Straus and Giroux, 1969). A thorough biography of Mark Rothko is James E. B. Breslin's *Mark Rothko: A Biography* (Chicago and London: University of Chicago Press, 1998). Dickinson's line on art's being a "gift of screws" appears in *The Poems of Emily Dickinson* (cited above).

TERRIBLE BEAUTY

John Keats's quotation on his life's being posthumous can be found in John Keats's *Selected Letters*, intro. Jon Mee and ed. Robert Gittings (Oxford, U.K., and New York: Oxford University Press, 2002), p. 369. The definitive biog-raphy of Keats is Walter Jackson Bates's *John Keats*, new ed. (Cambridge, Mass.: Belknap Press of Harvard University Press, 1979). Keats's quote on the "vale of Soul-making" can be found in *Selected Letters*, p. 232. His line on life as a "large Mansion of Many Apartments" can be found in the same publication, p. 89. Keats's great poem "Ode on Melancholy" appears in his *Selected Poems and Letters* (New York: Riverside Editions, 1959). Walker Percy's "The Loss of the Creature" can be found in Percy's *The Message in the Bottle: How Queer Man Is, How Queer Language Is, and What One Has to Do with the Other* (New York: Picador, 2000), pp. 46–63. My mention of *Mona Lisa* is based on Walter Benjamin's idea that art loses its sacred qualities in the age of mechanical reproduction. See his "The Work of Art in the Age of Mechanical Reproduction," in *Illuminations*, ed. Hannah Arendt and trans. Harry Zohn (cited above), pp. 217–52. My sentence on how many of us now eat menus instead of food is a rephrasing of a persistent claim of Alan Watts—that we in the Western world value abstract over concrete experience and thus value menus over food. This idea plays prominently in Watts's *Does It Matter? Essays on Man's Relation to Materiality* (New York: Vintage, 1971). My discussion of how Americans tend to reduce events of great import to idle talk has been influenced by Martin Heidegger's *Being and Time* (cited above). Heidegger also has seriously impacted my meditations on how anxiety leads us to consider our own deaths and thus to become authentic. See *Being and Time*, pp. 279–311. Beethoven's letter of 1787, the one on his chronic melancholia, is quoted in full in Lewis Lockwood's *Beethoven: The Music and the Life* (New York: Norton, 2003), pp. 3–4. Lockwood's biography of the composer helped me immensely. My meditations on Beethoven's melancholia were greatly influenced by William A. Frosch's "Moods, Madness, and Music. 1. Major Affective Disease and Musical Creativity," *Comprehensive Psychiatry* 28:4 (1987), pp. 315–22. Beethoven's quotation on how melancholy informed the largo of opus 10, number 3, appears in Frosch, p. 316. The letter in which Beethoven bids "defiance" to his "fate," though he is "God's most unhappy creature," is quoted in full in *Thayer's Life of Beethoven*, vol. 1, ed. and rev. Elliot Forbes (Princeton, N.J.: Princeton University Press, 1964), pp. 283–85. This still-definitive biography aided me considerably in my thinking about Beethoven. Beethoven's words on his desire to "seize Fate by the throat" are quoted in Lockwood, p. 215. The description of Beethoven's difficulty in hearing the shepherd pipe comes from Ferdinand Ries. This description can be found in *Beethoven: Impressions by His Contemporaries*, ed. O. G. Sonneck (New York: Dover, 1954), p. 56. Beethoven's famous Heiligenstadt confession can be found in *Thayer's Life*, pp. 304–306. Beethoven's remark on taking a new way can be found in Lockwood, p. 124. The vignette of Beethoven furiously composing can be found in Hershman and Lieb's *Manic Depression and Creativity*. Haydn's quotation on Beethoven's dark, strange music can also be found in this text. In my discussion of Friedrich von Schlegel's romantic irony, I draw from his *Philosophical Fragments*, trans. Peter Firchow (Minneapolis: University of Minnesota Press, 1991), pp. 36, 45. Excellent books on Romantic irony are Anne K. Mellor's *English Romantic Irony* (Cambridge, Mass.: Harvard University Press, 1980) and Philippe Lacoue-Labarthe and Jean-Luc Nancy's *The Literary Absolute: The Theory of Literature in German Romanticism*, trans. and intro. Philip Barnard and Cheryl Lester (Albany: State University of New York Press, 1988). Keats's quotation on negative capability can be found in John Keats's *Selected Letters* (cited above), p. 41. Keats on the poetical character's having no self appears in the *Letters*, pp. 147–48. My vignette on Cynthia Lennon discovering John and Yoko at her Weybridge house is based on Bob Spitz's *The Beatles: The Biography* (New York: Little, Brown, 2005), p. 772. I based my lines on John and Yoko's initial meeting on Mikal Gilmore's 2005 *Rolling Stone* article "John Lennon Lives Forever." A good book on the Fluxus movement, with which Ono was associated, is Hannah Higgins's *Fluxus Experience* (Berkeley: University of California Press, 2002). Ono's *Ceiling Painting* can be found in the Japan Society Gallery, New York City. Lennon's quotation on his pain and its connection to needing gods can be found in Gilmore's *Rolling Stone* article, as is his quotation on the trauma of losing his mother. For a thorough account of Lennon's ironic antics with Ono, see Ray Coleman's *Lennon: The Definitive Biography*, rev. ed. (New York: Harper, 1992). Lennon's letter to the queen can be found in Coleman, p. 510. *John Lennon/Plastic Ono Band* came out with EMI in 1970. Gilmore's lines on Lennon's "God" can be found in his 2005 *Rolling Stone* article. Friedrich von Schiller's thoughts on play appear in *Letters Upon the Aesthetic Education of Man*, trans. and intro. Reginald Snell (New York: Frederick Ungar, 1965), pp. 64–68, 74–80. A good biography of Handel is Donald Burrows's *Handel* (Oxford, U.K.: Oxford University Press, 1994). The definitive biography of Virginia Woolf is Hermione Lee's *Virginia Woolf* (New York: Vintage, 1999). A good biography of Georgia O'Keeffe is Roxana Robinson's *Georgia O'Keeffe: A Life* (London: Bloomsbury, 1990). The quotations from Thoreau came from *Walden; or, Life in the Woods* in *The Portable Thoreau* (New York: Viking, 1964), pp. 263, 557.

CONCLUSION

The Philip K. Dick novel I have in mind in my discussion of a "police state of Pollyannas" is *Flow My Tears, the Policeman Said* (London: Gollancz Press, 2001). Of course much of Dick's work deals with dystopias based on a collective desire for superficial happiness. For instance, see *Do Androids Dream of Electric Sheep?* (New York: Del Rey, 1996) and "We Can Remember It for You Wholesale," in *The Collected Stories of Philip K. Dick*, vol. 2 (New York: Citadel Press, 1998).

Acknowledgments

I am deeply indebted to several people who helped me transfer sullen ideas into readable prose. I would especially like to thank my wonderful agent, Bridget Wagner of the Sagalyn Literary Agency. Without her guidance, the book simply would not exist. From the earliest stages of the proposal to the last stages of editing, she provided indispensable advice and much-needed encouragement. I would also like to offer special thanks to Sarah Crichton, my editor at Farrar, Straus and Giroux. Sarah's brilliant insights into our current cultural condition and her keen sense of literary style improved my writing mightily at all stages of composition. I can't imagine a better editor. I also appreciate two close friends who were kind enough to read the book closely and to comment honestly on its strengths and weaknesses: Philip Kuberski, who has long been my intellectual mentor; and Philip Arnold, who for years has attuned me to the nuances of language. I was also assisted greatly by Stephen Corey, the acting editor of *The Georgia Review*. He helped me in deepening and polishing an essay, published in *The Georgia Review*, that turned out to be the seed of this book. I'm also thankful for rich conversations with four friends: Ken Cooper, John McNally, Dennis Sampson, and Marilyn Gaull. Each helped me to understand more deeply the nature of melancholy and the difficulties of writing about the mood. I'd also like to express appreciation to my parents, Glenn Wilson and Linda Wilson. Both have supported my endeavors immeasurably throughout my life; they have been especially patient with my chronic gloom. I'd also like to offer copious thanks to my wife, Sandi Hamilton, for her acute editorial help, for her inspiring words, and for her remarkable endurance of my melancholy moods. Most of all, though, I'd like to thank my daughter, Una. Though only five years old, she has, without even trying, consistently brightened my heart and made life worth living.

Printed in the USA
CPSIA information can be obtained
at www.ICGtesting.com
LVHW091134150724
785511LV00001B/136